The Quest for Perfection:

Shelley and the Poet-Hero

The Quest for Perfection:
Shelley and the Poet-Hero

SHEILAH R. CRAFT

Little Butterfly

Little Butterfly

Copyright © 2013 by Sheilah R. Craft

All rights reserved

Manufactured in the United States of America

Registered with the US Library of Congress

All rights reserved. No part of this book may be reproduced or transmitted in any form whatsoever without prior written permission from the publisher, except for brief quotations embodied in critical articles and reviews.

ISBN-13: 978-0615839158

ISBN-10: 0615839150

For

Ariel,

With Gratitude

CONTENTS

I	Introduction	1
II	The Revolutionary Ideal:	
	Shelley and the Perfect World	5
III	The Ideal Mate:	
	Shelley and Women	37
IV	Poet and Prophet:	
	Shelley and Poetry	65
V	The Ideal Relationship:	
	The Poet and Nature	69
VI	The Lifting of the Veil:	
	Death and the Poet	101
	Notes	111
	Works Consulted	115
	Acknowledgments	117

I: Introduction

Throughout his short yet prolific life and career, Shelley constantly searched for what he could never find--perfection.[1] This lifelong quest for perfection, in both society and his personal life, influenced every aspect of his life and career. His belief in the perfectibility of mankind, and of the world, as well as his desire for a perfect mate, led him to suffer great disappointment and disillusionment when the people, objects, or ideas upon whom he had placed his idealistic, impossible expectations inevitably failed to live up to those expectations. This study focuses on the development and metamorphosis of this belief. Many of Shelley's works deal with the theme of searching for perfection: in some poems this search is conducted via visions or trances during which the Poet (or protagonist) travels to other worlds; other poems are based upon actual relationships in Shelley's life and represent not only the search but also the subsequent disillusionment; still others are biographical, and show Shelley's growing belief that true perfection is found not in human relationships, or even in abstract ideas, but in Nature.

Shelley sought perfection everywhere: in ideas, in people, and in art. As his search continued, he turned from the appendages of the world and began seeking the elusive perfection increasingly in Nature. As both the man and his poetry matured, Shelley came to believe that mankind--as represented most often by the Poet-Hero persona--could find perfection only in death. Shelley's ultimate belief, as a man and as a poet, was that in death, when one is entombed within the earth, one does truly become enjoined with Nature and therefore assume the perfection of Nature, thus attaining perfection oneself. In death, as well, one does truly discover the truths and mysteries of existence, of life, of death, and even of life after death; death itself providing answers to the questions raised and encountered in the pursuit of perfection.

The purpose of this study is to examine and explore Shelley's search for perfection in the areas he sought it most desperately: in society, or, the world of man; in his relationships with women; in Nature; in his own work; and, ultimately, in death. Shelley created ideal situations and people in his imagination and in his work, and longed to bring his unrealistic ideals into reality. To Shelley, the perfect world was ruled by a true democracy, full of freedom and equality for all races and sexes, and free from cruelty, hatred, and revenge. He desired to bring this perfect world into existence by instigating bloodless revolutions which would, in turn, effect the changes he desired for mankind.

In his personal life, Shelley needed, indeed, almost demanded, a perfect female as his mate; unable to find such a being, he tried to recreate and mold impressionable young women into his ideal. However, his failure to realize that people are not perfect and completely good, and that they cannot be completely controlled and shaped by another, led him to certain heartbreak and disappointment when his illusions were ultimately shattered.

Shelley also projected his ideals onto Nature, creating his own perfect Nature in his imagination and in his works. Like his perfect society, Shelley's Nature is an impossibility, free of all darkness, cruelty, and evil.

THE QUEST FOR PERFECTION

A true perfectionist, Shelley even strove to create perfect art; a study of his manuscript notebooks reveals that he revised and rewrote his works many times, sometimes even after publication. This need to accomplish what he considered perfect poetry was, I feel, one of the reasons Shelley was such a prolific writer: never satisfied that he had achieved artistic perfection, he was driven to keep writing until he had, at least in his own mind, accomplished his goal. Shelley did, indeed, finally achieve that perfection in 1821, with the composition of <u>Adonais</u>, and the implications of that self-analysis shall also be explored.

Finally, Shelley considered death to be the supreme state of perfection, and his view of, and obsession with, death shall be examined; in light of his personal beliefs concerning death, the implications of Shelley's own death, at the age of 29, are thus relevant and shall be scrutinized. By studying the course of Shelley's pursuit of perfection, the reader shall come to recognize that this desperate longing for perfection fueled every aspect of Shelley's life, and that, while he hoped for success in bringing his ideals to fruition, Shelley was ultimately doomed to failure.

§§§§

Percy Bysshe Shelley was born into a life of wealth and privilege. The first ten years of his life were spent in the free and idyllic setting of the family estate, Field Place, in the small town of Horsham, Sussex. As a boy, Shelley's was the perfect existence; he grew up relatively wild and free, as wild and free as the nature which surrounded him. For a boy with an overactive and rich imagination, his life truly was the perfect life. However, his life and world would change forever at the age of ten, when his parents sent him away to school for the formal education and discipline that had been lacking in his early life. Introduced to the structure and caste system of Syon House Academy, Shelley rebelled, refusing to conform to the ways of the world. His time at school--at Syon House, then at Eton--was far from pleasant; indeed, he suffered in silence until he entered University College, Oxford, where he enjoyed more freedom than had previously been allowed him as a student. At Oxford, he was able to pursue in relative peace and solitude the interests and passions which grasped hold of his mind, namely scientific experiments and spiritual questions. At Oxford, Percy Shelley's search for perfection--perhaps to regain the perfection of his life at Field Place--began in earnest. This search would obsess him for the remainder of his short, dynamic life; it would become the underlying theme of many of his writings, and would determine the course of his actions.

II: The Revolutionary Ideal: Shelley and the Perfect World

Early in his life, Shelley became dissatisfied with the institutions of his native England--namely, government and religion--and designed to transform them into the perfect institutions he envisioned. Government and religion should not, he felt, be controlled by a monarch and his court, but should be influenced by a true democracy. The people should not be told what to think, feel, or do; rather, they should be free to come to their own conclusions on all matters--especially religion--and should be allowed to follow those conclusions. Shelley believed that all people deserved a perfect world, a world filled with freedom, equality, and love. In order to bring that perfect world into existence, the people would need to believe, as Shelley did, that the perfectibility of mankind, and of the world, was possible. Only then could the ideal, bloodless revolution which Shelley desired begin, eradicating all evil and tyranny from the world and from human beings.

Shelley's belief in the perfectibility of mankind, and of the world, rejected the existence of evil. Shelley believed that evil was not an inherent part of mankind, nor of the world. Evil was the creation of Satan, who tempted mankind with promises of wealth and power; by falling prey to Satan's promises, mankind allowed evil to be introduced into the world. Mankind ceased to be perfect once evil became part of it. It was Shelley's belief that evil could be purged from mankind and its world just as it had been introduced: by tempting mankind with visions of what it, and its world, could be once restored to a state of perfection, thus prompting mankind to resist evil. Not realizing that perfection was impossible to achieve in the world of man, Shelley continued to hope that his ideal would become a reality. Shelley assigned himself the mission of changing the people of the world, so that they, in turn, could change the world.

Shelley entered on his self-assigned mission in his late teens, while a student at Oxford, when he became frustrated with the system of government in England. He objected to the absolute rule of both the monarchy and Parliament, which controlled, in essence, every aspect of society, including religion. His attempt to challenge the men who ruled the church caused his expulsion from Oxford on March 25, 1811, for composing, with Thomas Jefferson Hogg, a pamphlet titled <u>The Necessity of Atheism</u>. As his cousin Charlotte Grove would write in her diary for April 2, she was "*sorry to hear Bysshe was expelled Oxford for writing to the Bishops on Atheism*" (Hawkins 83). In fact, the essay is actually a treatise against "*clerical deism*" (Cameron 73), more so than a blatant statement of disbelief in a supreme Deity. Shelley sent the pamphlet to the clergy for the purpose of garnering their responses to its contents; when it fell into the hands of the Oxford officials, it signaled the end of his (and Hogg's) career at the college. Shelley and Hogg, however, would have been allowed to remain at Oxford, had they only admitted to writing the essay and stated that they had erred in doing so and did not really believe their own words. Shelley never denied co-authoring the essay, but he refused to compromise his beliefs and deny that they were, in fact, his own. Thus, because he stood up for his convictions, he was expelled. If nothing else, this episode proves that Shelley almost always remained true to his beliefs, refusing to compromise them, and that he was willing to suffer any punishment on their behalf. In this respect, his calls for the people to stand tall and brave against the tyrants, in later works such as <u>Laon and Cythna</u> and "The Mask of Anarchy," have greater authority, stemming as they do from his own experiences.

Shelley continued to be an anti-establishment radical, calling on the people to take a stand against the government and to thus create a perfect state, populated by perfect human beings. The perfectibility of mankind, and of the world, was to be the subject of Shelley's first revolutionary poem. After writing a political pamphlet titled <u>Proposal for Putting Reform to the Vote,</u> it seems natural that the poem which followed it was one of Shelley's most overtly political poems. Originally titled <u>Laon and Cythna</u>, after the hero and heroine, it was Shelley's longest poem, the final word count being well over four thousand words. The cornerstone for this work was the French Revolution, an event which shaped much of Shelley's thinking. Shelley was greatly influenced by the radical writings of William Godwin, Mary Wollstonecraft, and Thomas Paine, whose ideas of equality and freedom were the basis for Shelley's own ideas. Godwin, Wollstonecraft, and Paine--as well as Shelley--objected to the fact that the people of France had been encouraged to revolt before they fully understood what freedom and equality truly meant; these writers felt that the people had not been prepared for the promised liberties, that they had been rashly rushed into the revolution, and were thus destined to fail. As we shall later see, Shelley especially believed that people had to be fully prepared for freedom, first by learning exactly what freedom entails--its responsibilities and rights, for example--before they could ever attempt to obtain it. White tells the story of an encounter Shelley had with a victim of the revolution while on a trip during the summer of 1814, an elderly man whose children had been murdered by the Cossacks. This encounter made Shelley see, for the first time, the effects of war, and was an experience which remained ingrained in his memory. In fact, this episode was to inspire Shelley's preface to <u>Laon and Cythna</u> (166).

The preface of Shelley's poem is as much a call to action as is the poem itself; in it, Shelley states his reasons for composing the poem and his desires for the change which the revolution would bring about. He tells us that he wishes to ignite within the bosoms of [his] readers a virtuous enthusiasm for those doctrines of liberty and justice, that faith and hope in something good, which neither violence nor misrepresentation nor prejudice can ever totally extinguish among mankind.

For this purpose [he has] chosen a story of human passion in its most universal character. . . . [He] would only awaken the feelings, so that the reader should see the beauty of true virtue, and be incited to those inquiries which have led to [his] moral and political creed, and that of some of the sublimest intellects in the world. . .(Shelley 32-34).

Shelley's desire, then, as a political poet, was to provoke people into questioning the systems of government; to arouse their interest in past political works--such as Godwin's or Paine's--and to thus realize that the ideal revolution of Shelley's poem could indeed come to fruition. The interest of the people would be garnered by Shelley's tale of two young revolutionaries, a story Shelley hoped would speak to the hearts, emotions, and passions of the people, prompting them to follow the lead of Laon and Cythna. Shelley, being a voracious reader and student, a sympathetic companion to Nature, and an empathetic and sympathetic political and social reformer, was the perfect poet to compose such a human, yet admittedly violent, story, though the violence was "*relieved by milder pictures of friendship and love, and natural affections*" (Ingpen 2: 559).

Shelley was, in fact, calling for the perfect revolution in his poem, an impossible and unrealistic revolution. While Shelley was realistic enough to recognize that violence would occur in a revolution, he was far more idealistic, truly believing and hoping that political and social changes could be obtained and maintained without violence and bloodshed. Shelley's peaceful revolution was an unrealistic ideal. As he says in his preface to Laon and Cythna, the revolution in this poem "*is the beau ideal, as it were, of the French Revolution*" (Ingpen 2: 559), a revolution based upon the goodness in mankind. Shelley thus denied the dark side of mankind, almost to the point of denying the existence of evil; in his ideal world, people were only good, and thus perfect, consequently making their systems and productions equally good and therefore perfect.

Laon and Cythna were, in fact, the perfect hero and heroine. Indeed, Laon mirrors Shelley, for he was, as Godwin Shelley says, a youth nourished in dreams of liberty, some of whose actions [we]re in direct opposition to the opinions of the world; but who [was] animated throughout by an ardent love of virtue, and a resolution to confer the boons of political and intellectual freedom on his fellow creatures (Shelley 154).

Laon was a young man deeply devoted to his beliefs and the cause of liberty and freedom, though, as Shelley stated in his preface, he realized that the sort of change which Laon (and Shelley) desired cannot occur overnight. Shelley, as we have seen, realized that newly-freed men would need time to adjust their minds, their habits, and their beliefs to their new situations, that at first they may be too overcome with emotion and too unused to freedom to behave as 'civilized' men. Shelley reiterated this realization in his note to the poem, when he stated, "*I am aware, methinks, of a slow, gradual, silent change. In that belief I have composed the following Poem*" (Shelley 34). Like Shelley, his hero recognized the fact that men released from years of tyranny, oppression and slavery would need time to adjust to freedom of thought and action.

His partner, Cythna, was of the same mold: she was an "*enlightened 'new woman'*" (Cameron, Circle 2: 921), the ideal woman who understood, sympathized with, and shared Laon's beliefs, ideas, and ideals. They were young revolutionaries who were willing to stand up for their beliefs and who were, in fact, willing to die for them. They were Shelley's perfect pair, created out of his own set of beliefs and convictions.

In the original poem, fully titled <u>Laon and Cythna; or, The Revolution of the Golden City: A Vision of the Nineteenth Century</u>, the hero and heroine were also brother and sister, as well as lovers. Perhaps because Shelley had been closest to his own sister, Elizabeth, as a youth and an adolescent, he felt that the brother-sister relationship was one of the truest and closest human relationships one could experience. Indeed, Elizabeth was, in many ways, his closest companion during those early years, and he felt that she understood and sympathized with him completely--a necessity in Shelley's relationships, as we shall later see. In light of the fact that Shelley's first close relationship was with his sister, one is not surprised that he chose to explore the complete spectrum of the brother-sister relationship in his poem. However, the incest, combined with Shelley's radical and controversial religious and political passages, about "*God, Hell, Christ, republicanism and atheism*" (Holmes 391), made for a potent and dangerous work. His publisher, Charles Ollier, feared persecution--not uncommon in the literary world of 1817; after all, writers who spoke out against the establishment were routinely imprisoned. In fact, Shelley had come to know Leigh Hunt when he was imprisoned for his blasphemous remarks against the Prince Regent in his newspaper; Shelley, predictably, supported Hunt, and they became lifelong friends. In light of this threat, not only to himself but to Ollier as well, Shelley finally relented to revise the text--but not until several copies had been printed, at his expense, and a few had reached the populous.

    When the work reappeared, it bore the title, <u>The Revolt of Islam</u>, and none of the offending passages. Laon and Cythna were now cousins, making their sexual union less shocking to the average reader; perhaps Shelley now took his inspiration from his adolescent romance with his cousin, Harriet Grove. The religious and political passages were greatly toned down as well, or, as Holmes says, "*much that had been politically explicit was now weakened and obscured*" (391). The poem opens with an autobiographical dedication to Mary Wollstonecraft Godwin Shelley, in which Shelley praises her as his ideal mate and blesses the day she entered his life. Stanza 8 of the dedication voices Shelley's belief that the child of two great minds--William Godwin and Mary Wollstonecraft--which he greatly admired would have to be great, intellectual and sympathetic herself. In Shelley's mind, Mary Godwin had to be full of promise and intellect--they were her birthright. She was left to develop under the guiding glow of her dead mother's greatness and her father's famous name. Such a creature as the daughter of Godwin and Wollstonecraft, he reasoned, had to be his perfect partner—presumably inheriting talent, intellect, compassion, understanding, and liberal ideas from her parents--and Shelley considered her such, at least in the early years of their relationship.

The story of Laon and Cythna, and the revolution, begins in Canto I, where the struggle between the revolution and the oppression it desires to crush is told through the allegorical tale of a battle between a snake--the symbol of the revolution--and an eagle--symbolizing the oppression. Shelley had decided to construct his own system of symbols, which would, he hoped, appeal to the peoples' collective imagination, and thus supplement the language he used to tell his story (White 247). It was for this reason that Shelley deliberately chose to reverse the symbols of good and evil; by doing so, he undoubtedly confused many readers, though he achieved his goal in making them think for themselves in order to understand the meanings of the symbols and of the passage. Just as is usually the case, however, Revolution is

THE QUEST FOR PERFECTION

injured and temporarily suppressed by Oppression, which has momentary victory.

Cantos II-IV contain the somewhat-fictionalized story of Shelley's own years of persecution as an adolescent and young adult, in which Laon represents Shelley. Laon even meets and befriends an "*aged man*" (line 1693) who is based on an early influence in Shelley's own life. As Godwin Shelley would later recall, Shelley came to know Dr. Lind while at Eton, a man who was, to Shelley, the perfect elderly man. Shelley himself would say that his debt to Dr. Lind was inestimable, for this man had given him far more than even Shelley's own father had; as Shelley stated, "*he loved me, and I shall never forget our long talks, where he breathed the Spirit of the kindest tolerance and the purest wisdom*" (Cameron, Circle 2: 637). Once again, we have a person who had entered Shelley's life, as had Harriet Grove, Harriet Westbrook, Elizabeth Hitchener, and Godwin Shelley, and who had given him the love, understanding, encouragement and sympathy which he craved; because of this, more so than for any other reason, Shelley responded to Dr. Lind, and placed him on a pedestal of reverence, respect and love. Lind was, as Shelley's words reveal, one of those ideal beings--just as the women in his life had each, alternately, seemed to be--with whom Shelley longed to surround himself. Dr. Lind died in 1813, and Shelley memorialized him as Laon's friend who "*wound [Laon] in his arms with tender care, / and very few, but kindly words. . .*" (lines 1424-1425).

The story of the revolution continues, in Canto V, with the taking of the city by the army of revolutionaries, led by Laon, who, like the serpent, is wounded. Canto VI sees the taking and destruction of the city by the Tyrant's army, who murder nearly all of Laon's followers, a passage which "marks what Shelley saw as the almost inevitable counter-reaction of violent revolution" (Holmes 394). In other words, without love and compassion, violence begets violence and murder breeds murder, in a never-ending cycle of hatred and revenge. Laon, one of the survivors, is rescued by Cythna, who charges in on a glorious steed, and they ride off to a "*ruin*" (line 2616), where, seated on a sofa of fallen leaves, they consummate their love while they are illuminated by "a wandering Meteor by some wild wind sent" (line 2617). Interestingly, Nature provides the setting for their love scene, as opposed to the cities of mankind.

Following the tender love scene, Cythna relates her own story of capture, imprisonment, and ultimate escape. Her story fills Cantos VII, VIII, and most of IX. At the end of Canto IX, Laon, horrified by her story, cries out in typical Shelleyan fashion, with an "*impassioned paean of hope and love*" (Holmes 396). After his passionate outburst, Cythna "*turned to [Laon] and smiled--that smile was Paradise!*" (line 3792). In her complete, true, passionate love and sympathy, he glimpses perfection.

The focus changes, in Canto X, to the people of the city, who are forced to live under the oppressive rule of the Tyrant. Echoing the Biblical stories Shelley had lately been reading, the people are beset and "*destroyed by plagues and famines and droughts, while their new rulers are reverting to the old superstitions of divine appeasement*" (Holmes 398). Once Laon discovers their fate, he decides to take up the fight in earnest yet again. At this point, Shelley's poem becomes darkest, full of grim images and language. As Holmes explains, the point of the poem is to show Shelley's "*rejection of the French*

THE QUEST FOR PERFECTION

Revolution as a model for further political and social change" (400). This is all part of Shelley's plan to change the thinking of the people first, for he realized that minds had to be changed before rules and establishments could be effectively changed. Otherwise, as we have seen, disaster befalls the people, and the revolution becomes bloody--as had the French Revolution.

After Laon fights for his cause once more, and becomes a vital threat to the Tyrant's army, his and Cythna's deaths are plotted by the Tyrant. Canto X ends with the pyre being built. Realizing their fate, Canto XI tells us, Laon leaves Cythna in the mountains, and gives himself up to the Tyrant in exchange for the promise of her safety; indeed, he prepares for his fiery death, thinking her on her way to

> *. . . a People mighty in its youth,*
>
> *A land beyond the Oceans of the West,*
>
> *Where, though with rudest rites, Freedom and Truth*
>
> *Are worshipped; from a glorious Mother's breast,*
>
> *Who, since high Athens fell, among the rest*
>
> *Sate like the Queen of nations. . .*
>
> *That land is like an Eagle. . .*
>
> (4414-4419, 4423)

Interestingly, Cythna is to be sent to America, the seat of democracy and freedom for all--the country whose Declaration of Independence and Bill of Rights were the model for much of Shelley's political thinking and writings.

The story continues in Canto XII, when, thinking his lover safely on her way to a new land, Laon is bound to the stake as a throng of silent witnesses watches the executioner's preparations. Just as one would expect from Shelley, Cythna comes riding in on her giant steed yet again, not to save Laon, but to join him at the stake. The two young lovers die together, in one of the most beautiful death scenes ever written, a death scene full of love and the promise of perfection; as Laon says,

> *She smiled on me, and nothing then we said,*
>
> *But each upon the other's countenance fed*
>
> *Looks of insatiate love; the mighty veil*
>
> *Which doth divide the living and the dead*
>
> *Was almost rent, the world grew dim and pale,--*
>
> *All light in Heaven or Earth beside our love did fail.*
>
> (4579-4584)

As they die, the veil between life and death is torn apart, and they are shown what the future holds for them: perfection. Canto XII concludes with an epilogue of twenty-five stanzas, an epilogue which sees the hero and heroine beginning their new, postmortem existence together.

Laon opens the epilogue by asking, in wonderment, "*and is this death?*" (line 4594), a question which clearly tells the reader that death is certainly not what he had expected it to be. He and Cythna are reclining "*on the waved and golden sand / of a clear pool, upon a bank o'ertwined / with strange and star-bright flowers, which to the wind / breathed divine odour*" (lines 4605-4608), surrounded by "*lawny mountain*" (line 4612), forests and caves. As a boat made of pearl approaches, steered by a "*plumed Seraph*" (line 4657), Cythna cries out, "*Ay, this is Paradise / and not a dream, and we are all united!*" (lines 4643-4644). In stanza 38, we are told that their journey lasts three days and three nights, whereupon their boat rests "*on a line suspended / between two heavens*" (lines 4805-4806), and Laon looks off into the distance and sees, for the first time, their new home, which is the "*Temple of the Spirit*" (line 4815). Laon and Cythna are, indeed, in Paradise. By standing up for their beliefs and fighting for their cause, for remaining true to their love of freedom and of one another, for dying for the revolution and for their love, they have received the ultimate reward. In death, they are given new life in Paradise, a place where there is no famine nor murder. Their vision may not as yet have come true on earth, but they shall spend all of eternity enveloped in their own Elysian universe. In death, they have found the perfect world.

<u>Laon and Cythna</u> is important for many reasons: like all of his work, it records Shelley's thoughts and beliefs at the time of composition, and it speaks to a cause very important to Shelley as a human being--the equality and freedom of all human beings. This poem also speaks to a theme which shall be explored in detail later, that of death as the provider of the ultimate state of perfection. Most importantly, however, this poem, more than any other, illustrates what to Shelley was the perfect revolution. Unlike the Tyrant's army, Laon and his followers never revert to violence and bloodshed to achieve their goals. Bloodshed was what Shelley wanted, more than anything else, to avoid; for him, a bloodless revolution was

the perfect revolution, though, as we have seen, an unrealistic revolution. As he stressed in the preface of his poem, he knew that one first had to effect change in the peoples' minds before one could affect permanent political change.

Shelley continued to hope that his ideal, perfect, bloodless revolution would occur, and thus bring about the perfect world. In his poetry, he continued to speak out against the violence enacted against the people by those such as the Tyrant. Such violence and bloodshed were the inspiration for Shelley's next political poem, "The Mask of Anarchy," composed in September of 1819. On August 16, 1819, in St. Peter's Field, Manchester, a rally in support of Parliamentary reform was held, and attended by peaceful men, women, and children. The figures vary, but at least six people were killed and eighty wounded, when "*a group of drunken militia and cavalrymen misinterpreted their orders and charged into*" the crowd (Reiman Poetry and Prose 301). When Shelley, living in Italy, heard of the bloody event, it angered and sickened him. As he wrote to Charles Ollier on September 6, his indignation was at a fever pitch, and he anxiously waited to hear England's reaction to this needless violence on the part of the soldiers (Ingpen 2: 716). Three days later, on September 9, Shelley wrote to his friend Peacock that the violence represented the distant thunders of the terrible storm which is approaching. *"The tyrants here, as in the French Revolution, have first shed blood. May their execrable lessons not be learnt with equal docility!"* (Ingpen 2: 718).

As this letter illustrates, Shelley was afraid that the people would take the easy route to freedom, and copy the violent behavior of their oppressors. The result would, of course, be just what Shelley wanted to prevent: a bloody, murderous uprising. Shelley hoped the people would turn to men such as himself and Paine for the answers, thus learning that violence was not the means for accomplishing permanent freedom.

In "The Mask of Anarchy", Shelley was responding to the very violence Laon and Cythna fought against in the earlier poem. His letter to Peacock makes clear his steadfast devotion to the beau ideal, the perfect, bloodless revolution he had provided the blueprints for in The Revolt of Islam. In her note to "The Mask of Anarchy," Godwin Shelley explains that

> *he was a republican, and loved democracy. He looked on all human beings as inheriting an equal right to possess the dearest privileges of our nature; the necessaries of life when fairly earned by labour, and intellectual instruction. . . . [The Manchester Massacre] roused in him violent emotions of indignation and compassion. The great truth that the many, if accordant and resolute, could control the few, as was shown some years after, made him long to teach his injured countrymen how to resist.*

(Shelley 341-342)

Shelley, moved and touched by the violence of the massacre, as well as of the French Revolution, resolved to do what he could to prevent such violence from occurring again. In order to provide his fellow beings with the freedom and equality which were the cornerstones of democracy, he felt it his duty, through his writings, to instruct people how to remain steadfast to their goals, preferably as a united force.

Because this poem was, as Godwin Shelley goes on to say, written for the general public, rather than for the esoteric few Shelley claimed many of his poems were composed, it is in a form unusual for him--it is a satire, which depicts all the worst traits of those in charge of England's government, including religion. For example, Lord Castlereagh is called "*Murder*" (line 5); as Reiman explains, Castlereagh, the Foreign Secretary and Tory leader of the House of Commons, "*had earlier been infamous for his bloody suppression of unrest in Ireland; now Shelley (and Byron) blamed him for his support of Austria and the reactionary Holy Alliance in Europe*" (Poetry and Prose 301). A personal note sounds when Shelley calls Baron Eldon, then the Lord Chancellor, "*Fraud*" (line 14); Eldon had refused to grant Shelley custody of his two young children by his first wife when she committed suicide, and this act Shelley never forgot nor forgave. Anarchy--political disorder and violence--is then personified in language reminiscent of the book of Revelation:

> . . .*he rode*
>
> *On a white horse, splashed with blood;*
>
> *He was pale even to the lips,*
>
> *Like Death in the Apocalypse.*
>
> *And he wore a kingly crown,*
>
> *And in his grasp a sceptre shone;*
>
> *On his brow this mark I saw--*
>
> '*I AM GOD, AND KING, AND LAW!*'
> (30-37)

THE QUEST FOR PERFECTION

These--God, King, and Law, or, rather, the rulers of church and state--are representatives of the tyrants and oppressors which Shelley longed to vanquish from seats of power and authority. In his opinion, these men had abused their power for their own benefit and to the detriment of the people. It was up to the people to rid their states of such rulers, and Shelley used his poetry to teach them how to vanquish the leaders of church and state.

These men shall be vanquished by the people, whom Shelley calls to action, imploring them to awaken, arise and intervene in history, and thus take control of their own fates:

> *'Men of England, heirs of Glory,*
>
> *Heroes of unwritten story,*
>
> *Nurslings of one mighty Mother,*
>
> *Hopes of her, and one another;*
>
> *'Rise like Lions after slumber*
>
> *In unvanquishable number,*
>
> *Shake your chains to earth like dew*
>
> *Which in sleep had fallen on you--*
>
> *Ye are many--they are few.*
>
> *'What is Freedom?--ye can tell*

That which slavery is, too well--

For its very name has grown

To an echo of your own.' (147-159)

Just as Shelley had previously stated his realization that political change could not occur without first changing the minds of men, he now warns the people that change is not always obvious, that it is often veiled by *"the dust of death"* (line 95). In other words, the people would have to be willing to sacrifice their own lives, as did the fictional Laon and Cythna, for the sake of the cause; though, ideally, they should never take another's life, Shelley believed that the people should have enough conviction to the cause to risk their own, individual lives for its furtherance. If the people were acting as one united, organized front, rather than as separate, disorganized individuals, their chances of successfully unseating the tyrants in charge were greater, and individual losses, though sad, would not be felt as sorely. As Shelley states in stanzas 56-63, the people of England, acting as one united force, will vanquish their tyrannical oppressors just as spring's winds blow away the skeletons of winter's long and cold season.

Once the tyrants are unseated, the people must use their tools--"*'Science, Poetry, and Thought'*" (line 254); their virtues--"*'Spirit, Patience, Gentleness'*" (line 258); and their medium--"*'a great Assembly'*" (line 262) like the one in Manchester--in order to remain the arbiters of their laws and the pilots of their fates. They will then have the perfect society, a democracy like that of the young America.

THE QUEST FOR PERFECTION

In his next revolutionary work, Shelley turned his talents once more to prose, writing what would be his longest political essay, A Philosophical View of Reform. Interestingly, at the same time he was writing his essay, Shelley was simultaneously working on his drama, Prometheus Unbound, a work which concerns equality for, and the perfectibility of, mankind. These works emphasize Shelley's belief that man's conscience would eventually resurface and institute the political and social changes he longed for. Following the bloody massacre of August 16, Shelley seemed more determined than ever to scatter his thoughts among mankind and to encourage the people to end oppression and domination. A perfect world is not based on an oppressive government, but rather a democratic government, a government truly by and for the people. Though Shelley's government was based upon the democracy of the young America, it was an idealized government; after all, not even America truly promised freedom and equality for all, but rather for a select group. As was typical of Shelley, he overlooked the flaws of American democracy and idealized the good in it. Thus, Shelley had created, in his mind and in his works, a system of government that was completely good and just; Shelley's perfect government was impossible to attain, a fact he failed to realize. His essay addressed not only the benefits of democracy, but also his belief that such drastic changes must be gradual, and without bloodshed; the Manchester Massacre; and the poet's role in such a reformation. Indeed, Shelley stated that, like Laon and Cythna, the people must be willing to face the tyrant's army and possible death for the sake of freedom and equality. The duty of poets, philosophers, and artists was to lead the people toward that freedom, a duty Shelley himself took very seriously. If his ideal world was to exist, peopled with perfect human beings, then his duty was to teach his fellow beings how to bring that world into existence.

Shelley's essay, in fact, echoes his earlier political poems, The Revolt of Islam and "The Mask of Anarchy," poems which outlined his plan for the political reformation his essay calls for. The Poet was to be no mere witness of the reformation and the revolution, though; he was to be a participant, indeed, the founder of the movement. The Poet was to teach and guide the people through his works, as Shelley had hoped to do via his poems and essays. The Poet's works would not only call the people to action, they would also instruct them in how to institute and affect a peaceful revolution and thus a perfect world. The revolutionary could, and should, be willing to die for his cause, but he should never willingly take the life of another fellow being. Shelley's political writings would, he hoped, instigate the movement toward the total perfection of the world, of mankind, and of art.[2]

Shelley closed his essay by stating that the works of great artists such as "*Godwin, Hazlitt, Bentham and Hunt . . . would be like a voice from beyond the dead of those who will live in the memories of men when they must be forgotten; it would be Eternity warning Time . . .*" (Woodring 488). Just as the soul is eternal, living forever after death, the words of great poets and writers will live forever, to be lessons for those who follow them on this earth. These great minds would therefore be able to guide mankind throughout the succeeding generations, helping them to not only achieve but maintain the perfect world. The realization that his words would become eternal, available to readers centuries after his own death, seemed to fit into Shelley's plan to change people's minds and attitudes, to bring about the peaceful revolution, and thus accomplish a state of perfection. To Shelley, Time was a redeemer, not an enemy, of mankind, and would teach it from the pages of history.

This idea was in Shelley's mind as he worked on his <u>Prometheus Unbound</u>, a work which he considered "*of a higher character than anything [he] ha[d] yet attempted, and is perhaps less an imitation of anything that ha[d] gone before it*" (Ingpen 2: 715). Shelley idealizes history, by emphasizing the good of both the world's and mankind's histories, for the benefit of expressing his belief in a Utopia, a perfect world. Shelley felt that if people were shown both the world and mankind at their best, they would then be motivated to change their own world and behavior, bringing out the good in themselves and burying the dark side. Once more, Shelley states his belief that perfection, however impossible it may appear, is indeed possible, and that "*man achieves freedom from evil only when he can rise above the feeling of revenge, which is in itself a self-perpetuating evil*" (White 321). In Shelley's version of the myth, Prometheus and his torture represent mankind's oppressive suffering at the hands of tyrants. Prometheus, like Laon and Cythna, was to be a model for mankind to follow; it was Shelley's wish that Prometheus' freedom from oppression, dominance, and slavery would inspire the people to work toward the perfect world he had long envisioned. Prometheus' freedom, then, represents freedom for all human beings. Interestingly, the gods punish Prometheus, causing the reader to equate them, in their glory and positions of power, with the rulers Shelley had long spoken out against. Jupiter--the "*tyrant of the world*" (III.iv.183)--is unseated and exiled, symbolic of Shelley's desire to free the world of tyrannical rulers. The drama closes not only with a celebration of Prometheus' freedom, but a discourse on how to regain freedom in the event mankind should lose it to tyrants in the future.

In his preface to the drama, Shelley speaks of his purpose in composing it and of his purpose as a poet, calling Prometheus the perfect man, a man motivated not by revenge, but rather by his desire to end suffering for all. As the author of the drama, Shelley's purpose was to introduce his readers to the idealistic, perfect state of mind and universe, his words and ideals becoming seeds scattered among the masses; it is the duty of the people to gather, plant and reap those seeds, thus following Shelley's doctrine. The harvest, Shelley says, will be happiness, for mankind will then have overcome the evil within and become perfect beings.

As he had stated in the Reform essay, his duty as a poet, as a spokesman for mankind, was to present it with tools which would better enable it to envision a perfect world and which would instruct it in how to accomplish that world; he had also mentioned that Time, or, history, was a great teacher of mankind, and that great minds, like Godwin, were the ones who most honestly recorded and preserved that history. In the Prometheus Unbound preface, he expounds upon the thoughts expressed in the essay, by stating that poetry gives man glimpses of Shelley's ideal, of his perfect world, in order to prepare the human mind once more for the ability to "*love, admire, trust, hope and endure*" (Shelley 203), making it possible for man to once more be the moral being he had been in the Garden of Eden. Shelley believed that that primordial being yet existed within his fellow beings; mankind was innately good, and could dispose of the world's evils if it so desired. As Godwin Shelley explains in her note to the poem,

> *the prominent feature of Shelley's theory of the destiny of the human species was that evil is not inherent in the system of the creation, but an accident that might be expelled. This also forms a portion of Christianity. . . . Shelley believed that mankind had only to will that there should be no evil, and there would be none. . . . Shelley loved to idealize the real. . . .*

(Shelley 267)

As his wife recognized, Shelley believed that evil was not a natural part of the human being nor of the world, and therefore, not of God's creation. As becomes evident when one probes into Shelley's desire for perfection, Shelley was unable to accept that evil is, indeed, a part of creation, and that it does innately exist within man and the world. Because he was unable to face evil, Shelley emphasized the good. This inability to acknowledge the dark, evil side of all creation is the fundamental flaw in Shelley's theory, a flaw which, as we shall see, condemned him to suffer disappointment and failure.

Shelley, however impossible his expectations were, continued to hope for the bloodless revolutions which would bring about freedom, equality, and thus the perfect world. In the spring of 1820, Shelley had the opportunity to celebrate the Spanish liberal revolution. When Napoleon invaded Spain in 1808, and placed his brother Joseph on the throne, the people of Spain and its territories rebelled. Though many lives were lost in the ensuing revolution, the Spanish territories did stand firm, and finally declared their independence from Spain (Adams, Briquebec, and Kramer 118-119). Though the loss of life was, of course, nothing to celebrate, the victory of the peoples' independence inspired Shelley to write the "Ode to Liberty," a "prayer to the goddess of Liberty" (Reiman 229), which tells the history of man and his great cities, Athens and Rome. Spain's victory urged the poet to call for more revolutionary change; the territories' hard-won independence filled him with the hope that others could learn from Spain's example and work toward their own freedom. While some interpreters question who Shelley is calling to action, stanza 13 proves that he is calling once more on the people of England, this time to follow Spain's example:

> *England yet sleeps: was she not called of old?*
>
> *Spain calls her now, as with its thrilling thunder*
>
> *Vesuvius wakens AEtna. . . .*
>
> *Her chains are threads of gold, she need but smile*
>
> *And they dissolve; but Spain's were links of steel,*
>
> *Till bit to dust by virtue's keenest file.*
>
> *Twins of a single destiny!* (181-183, 189-192)

Shelley is imploring the people of England to rise against their oppressive government--a monarchy--and to establish a democracy. This interpretation is supported by the opening lines of stanza 15, in which the anti-monarchist in Shelley speaks out, passionately hoping

> that the free would stamp the impious name

THE QUEST FOR PERFECTION

> Of King into the dust! or write it there,
>
> So that this blot upon the page of fame
>
> Were as a serpent's path, which the light air
>
> Erases, and the flat sands close behind! (211-215)

Once again, Shelley is stressing the importance of eliminating a government controlled by a monarch--likened to a serpent, the harbinger of sin and evil--and his chosen few. Shelley's perfect world was not ruled by a monarchy, but run by an elected democracy, or, at the least, a completely reformed Parliament. One country's victory in achieving a degree of liberation was a victory for Shelley, yet it was not enough. He still longed to free the people of his native England from the tyrants who were oppressing them; though he had been exiled from them, for both personal and political reasons, Shelley's concern and compassion for his countrymen had never diminished. He longed for them to have a perfect country, one free of tyrannical rulers and leaders; Shelley wanted the people of England to control their government, and thus their fates.

Shelley's poetry continued to focus on his desire for a perfect world and perfect human beings, proving that he remained true to his ideals. In August of 1820, Shelley composed <u>The Witch of Atlas</u>, a poem which seemingly contains no overtly heavy social or political themes or concerns--say, for example, like "The Mask of Anarchy." Following his somber political writings, though, and the many deeply serious and sometimes personal poems he had written in recent years (even his satires were political expositions), it seems likely that Shelley needed to release his tensions and emotions. This poem is "*a light-weight virtuoso piece*" (Holmes 607) which gave Shelley a chance to express his political and revolutionary ideas in a more lighthearted manner than was usual for him. Perhaps this "*wildly fanciful*" (Shelley 382) poem allowed Shelley to ease the burden he had placed upon himself. Though his Witch was to represent a divine creator of sorts, a creator of good and perfection, Shelley allowed himself to have some fun in composing this poem, something he normally denied himself. Shelley was perhaps too serious at most times, weighing his mind with political, social, and personal concerns to the point of exhaustion. His constant need to be enveloped in a perfect environment, and the burden of trying to maintain that perfection, was beginning to take its toll on his mental and physical health. He needed to ease his stress by creating a fanciful being such as the Witch.

The Witch is a vision of perfection, "*a lovely lady garmented in light / from her own beauty*" (lines 81-82), a beauty which is so rare that it causes men to come to her mountain cave and worship her. Her joy comes from visiting sleeping mortals, at which time she leaves them gifts according to their physical beauty; as White summarizes, the most beautiful are given immortality, tyrants are enabled to view themselves as the knaves they are, and the demure are released from their shyness (373). The reader, then, cannot deny that, in the end, Shelley's frivolous poem never strays too far from his long-standing concerns for the betterment of the world and of mankind. Though he was treating his subject in a manner more playful than he was accustomed to do, Shelley still wrote about the evils of the world, and of their effect upon mankind. Shelley's purpose remained the same, for he hoped to show the people how beneficial a world without evil, without oppression and slavery, would be, thus encouraging mankind to work toward that perfect world. The Witch becomes a type of deity, one who rewards or punishes people based on their deeds and attributes; as always in Shelley's world, the king, the priests, the miser and the soldier are given the worst fates. They are made fools and receive punishments which suit their crimes and misdeeds, usually ridiculing themselves, such as when

> The king would dress an ape up in his crown
>
> And robes, and seat him on his glorious seat,
>
> And on the right hand of the sunlike throne
>
> Would place a gaudy mock-bird to repeat
>
> The chatterings of the monkey. (633-637)

This stanza voices Shelley's view that monarchs are self-centered fools who surround themselves with subservient courtiers. Monarchs are in positions of power and authority, but they abuse that power and authority and trifle with peoples' lives. The Witch, in effect, usurps the King's power and causes him to toy with his own life, and thus see himself as others--such as Shelley--see him. With the king and his fellow tyrants stripped of their powers, and the people given their wondrous gifts, the Witch is able to create the perfect world. Though he had dealt with his concerns in a humorous manner, rather than in the overtly serious treatise he customarily composed, Shelley had once more succeeded in showing his readers what a world free of oppression and evil would be like.

Shelley's next work, however, was blatantly political--it was a celebration of a revolution in Naples in July of 1820. The hope Shelley had stated in the "Ode to Liberty" seemed to be coming true; "*the success of the Spanish insurgents stimulated the Neapolitans, [and] an incipient revolt broke out, which the soldiers of King Ferdinand refused to suppress. Most of the army went over to the revolution, and King Ferdinand was compelled to grant a constitution to Naples*" (White 374). In what could have very well been a script by Shelley himself, Sicily followed Naples' example; as Shelley wrote to Godwin Shelley on July 23, the event was not as pleasant, but the result was perfect: the people had banded together in their fight, and Sicily, too, was free (Ingpen 2: 807). Though the end was not to be as bloodless as Shelley would have preferred--the Austrians "*bloodily extinguished Neapolitan freedom within a few months*" (White 374)--Shelley was full of hope at the victories which were achieved, and thus composed his "Ode to Naples." This fully public poem speaks of the human desire for freedom which was then being felt, and of Shelley's hope that Naples, like Spain, would continue to influence the other states of Italy to instigate revolutions. Shelley ends his poem with a prayer to Love, asking this "*Great Spirit*" (line 149) to protect and encourage the cause of freedom and the revolutionaries fighting for it.

Love, to Shelley, was the driving force within man; man had only to call upon it and all feelings of hatred and revenge would be deadened. Also, once mankind let its love rule it, all forms of evil would be banished from the world, and Shelley's perfect world would come into existence. Indeed, Shelley never abandoned his belief that a perfect world was attainable, nor that the hearts of men could be made, once more, to feel love and compassion for their fellow beings. Though he remained idealistic in this regard, he was not naive: he knew that, until love and compassion took hold of mankind's hearts, victory--freedom--would be gained only at the expense of many lives. However, he hoped, as always, through his poetry, to guide people toward love and compassion, and thus a bloodless revolution, and never rejected the hope that peace would come without bloodshed.

Shelley's last major revolutionary poem, <u>Hellas</u>, composed in October 1821, was his response to the Greek fight for independence, and is similar in tone to <u>The Revolt of Islam</u> of 1817. Not only is the poem inspired by the Greek fight for independence, but, as Shelley states in the preface, also by the ancient Greek dramas, works which are, undeniably, considered the ideal, or, perfect, models which all dramatists look to for guidance; however, not only the dramas of the ancient Greeks are the perfect models, but all productions of the people of ancient Greece. As Shelley says, the perfection achieved by the Greeks shall continue to inspire mankind to aspire towards that perfection until the end of the human race (Shelley 441-442). Shelley, then, has taken the perfection of the ancient Greeks as his model, apparently feeling himself incapable of attaining poetic perfection yet again, as he felt he had with his previous poem, <u>Adonais</u>; this thought is expressed to John Gisborne in a letter dated October 22, 1821, in which he says that he was finishing <u>Hellas</u>, a "*sort of imitation of the 'Persae of AEschylus.*" Shelley next makes the revealing statement, "*I try to be what I might have been, but am not successful*" (Ingpen 2: 920). In fact, Shelley was becoming disillusioned with his role as a poet; his letters of early 1822 reflect much discontent for the poet and his last production, Hellas. On January 11, he wrote to Peacock that

> *[He] wish[ed he] had something better to do than furnish this jingling food for the hunger of oblivion, called verse, but [he did] not; and since [Peacock gave him] no encouragement about India, [he could not] hope to have.* (Ingpen 2: 929)

Peacock explains that the reference to India reflected Shelley's wish to be employed at the court of an Indian prince, but that such opportunities were not available to the average person (Ingpen 2: 929). The very fact that Shelley was exploring new career options indicates how weary he had become as a poet following the achievement of Adonais. On April 11, Shelley wrote to Horace Smith that his latest work "*is a poem written on the Greek cause last summer--a sort of lyrical, dramatic nondescript piece of business*" (Ingpen 2: 958). In an April 10 letter to John Gisborne, Shelley reveals that Hellas "*was written without much care, and in one of those few moments of enthusiasm which now seldom visits me, and which make me pay dear for their visits*" (Ingpen 2: 953), a remark which reveals that the act of creating poetry was not as effortless for him as it had previously been. This is not to suggest that Shelley was a muse of sorts, who dashed off lines of verse without thought or contemplation; in fact, as his manuscript notebooks and faircopies plainly reveal, Shelley was a serious artist, rewriting and revising his work throughout the process of composition and publication.

Shelley was a serious artist, an artist with a self-assigned and self-defined mission. That mission, as we have seen, was to bring into reality the idealistic, perfect world he had created in his mind and in his works. Too idealistic to realize that his perfect world was impossible to achieve, for it denied the existence of evil, Shelley was destined to suffer disappointment, heartbreak, and failure. Rather than simply imploring mankind to control his dark side, Shelley called for its complete eradication, which is itself impossible. As appealing as Shelley's perfect, idealized world appears, it is, in reality, unrealistic, a fact he never accepted nor acknowledged; this inability to recognize that evil was a natural part of all creation, condemned him, as we shall see, to finally seek perfection in death.

III: The Ideal Mate: Shelley and Women

In his personal world, as well as in mankind's world, Shelley constantly searched for perfection, in the guise of the ideal woman, the perfect partner. In striving to find that perfect female, Shelley turned to a succession of impressionable young women, whom he felt he could recreate and shape into his ideal. Just as he had longed to bring his perfect world into being, Shelley desired to have the ideal mate. Such a woman would have to understand, believe in, and sympathize with Shelley's own system of beliefs; she would possess complete understanding of, and sympathy with, Shelley as both a man and an artist, giving him the support and compassion he craved; she would be able to discern the beauty and goodness of creation, and support him in his efforts to bring that goodness to the forefront, repressing all evil under its ethereal glow; and, she would have to be mute and uncomplaining regarding life's misfortunes and tragedies, for, as we shall see, Shelley was unwilling to accept that life was, at times, unfair. His ideal woman would also have to be beautiful, as perfectly beautiful as an ancient Greek sculpture. She must also be intellectual, possessing a mind as great as his own, as well as a reader and, perhaps, a writer, herself. Most importantly, though, she would allow Shelley to completely instruct and guide her ideas and thoughts. Such a woman as Shelley envisioned did not exist, for, yet again, Shelley failed to realize that perfection was impossible; he thus set himself up for heartbreak and failure, though his pain never prompted him to completely abandon the search for the perfect partner. Shelley's quest for his ideal woman began in his adolescence, and was to obsess him for the remainder of his life.

Shelley's first romance, with his cousin, Harriet Grove, was a typical adolescent affair, with the obligatory exchange of love letters and visits to each other's homes. Shelley, at the age of 12, began writing poems dedicated to Grove, poems which hint at things to come; for example, in "To St. Irvyne," dated February 28, 1805, when Shelley was 13, he placed the poet and his young love amid the ruins of St. Irvyne near Horsham, and the beauties of Nature:

When with Harriet I sat on the mouldering height

When with Harriet I gazed on the star-spangled sky

And the August Moon shone thro' the dimness of night

(5-7, Reiman, Esdaile 190)

Grove is thus connected to the remnants of the past as well as the celestial entities, symbols which would recur in Shelley's poetry years later, again in reference to women. In the fifth stanza of this early poem, Grove is thought to have been a dream, a vision, as if she were too beautiful or perfect to have been real; thus, the moonlight visit to the ruin becomes a dream itself. The sixth and final stanza introduces the theme of death, a theme, as we shall see, which Shelley would explore with greater intensity in later works. The fact that, at such a young age, Shelley compared his love to a vision, and placed himself in the grave, are intriguing for the scholar interested in tracing Shelley's search for truth and perfection; the majority of his mature work would use the same imagery:

> *My Harriet is fled like a fast-fading dream*
>
> *Which fades ere the vision is fixed on the mind*
>
> *But has left a firm love and a lasting esteem*
>
> *That my soul to her soul must eternally bind*
>
> *When my mouldering bones lie in the cold, chilling grave*
>
> *When my last groans are borne o'er Strood's wide Lea*
>
> *And over my Tomb the chill night-tempests rave*
>
> *Then, loved Harriet, bestow one poor thought on me*

(17-24, Reiman, Esdaile 191)

Intriguingly, Grove is a "*fast-fading dream*" (line 17) which will flee and fade, leaving him behind to carry the memory of their romance to the grave. Shelley seems to realize, perhaps subconsciously, that the ideal Harriet of his poem will eventually cease to exist, that he will awaken, and that he would then have to seek perfection elsewhere--in this instance, in the grave, in death.

    The two families, the Shelleys and the Groves, understood that Bysshe (as his family called him) and Harriet were "engaged," and would marry as soon as they were of age. Both teenagers seemed pleased with this arrangement, and the parents encouraged their correspondence; in the beginning, this relationship appeared as normal as any adolescent romance. However, theirs was not exactly a normal romance. In fact, Shelley looked upon Grove as one who would allow him to "*convert [her] into [a] deist; 'divine little scion of infidelity'*" (Cameron 16), or, rather, as a "*potential initiate*" (Hawkins 55). Shelley had long possessed "*intellectual domination*" (Cameron 16) over his sisters, and had longed to convert them into deists, and he desired to have the same hold over Grove as well, thus molding them into perfect females: beings who agreed with and practiced his developing theories of free love and religion.³

A contemporary of Shelley's, Joseph Merle, would later recall an extraordinary plan of Shelley's to withdraw from the world with two young children, preferably female, whom he would rear in total innocence 'of religious or social government' and knowing 'nothing of men or manners' so that Shelley might eventually see 'what the impressions of the world are upon the mind when it had been fully veiled from human prejudice'. So original a scheme may perhaps be less original than it seems. Shelley could have adapted it from a plan conceived by Thomas Day, the author of <u>Sanford and Merton</u>. Day, an admirer of Rousseau, brought up an orphan blonde girl and a foundling brunette in absolute seclusion during the 1770s. In this case the intention was to produce in one or the other a 'child of Nature' as the perfect wife for himself, but the scheme failed to come to fruition. Shelley's later plan did not get beyond the first outline (Hawkins 55).

One finds in Merle's recollections evidence that Shelley had, in his teens, begun to turn from the world of man in his search for the ideal being. In Shelley's opinion, society fostered the cruelty and hatred--the dark side--within mankind. In order to eradicate that evil side of man, Shelley felt it necessary to raise children outside the society of man; such people would therefore, he reasoned, be free from evil. Intriguingly, Shelley proposed to escape society with two female children, leading one to conclude that his intention was to create his ideal woman. Shelley, like Day, was also an admirer of Rousseau, and derived much of his Romanticism from the Frenchman's writings. Shelley, then, would have most likely been aware of Rousseau's Emile, in which he outlines the upbringing of the perfect being, one more a child of Nature than of society. Even though Shelley never acted out his plan, the relevance is that he was, even while still a teenager, contemplating the creation of children of Nature and the perfect mate. These ideas, as we shall see, were to remain with Shelley throughout his life.

In his attempt to convert Grove into a deist, and thus mold her into his ideal, Shelley, in the autumn of 1810, wrote letters to Grove which were most likely "*full of revolutionary ideas of all sorts*" (Hawkins 54). While none of those letters has survived, Cameron states that those letters were, indeed, "anti-religious [in] nature" (72-73), and certainly helped put a final end to the relationship between Shelley and Grove. Shelley was, however, becoming disillusioned with Grove, for she proved to be an unwilling subject, one uninterested in his ever-broadening interests (Hawkins 60-61). Grove was a disappointment for Shelley, for she proved to be merely human after all, and not the pliable, ideal woman he had hoped to produce. She steadfastly refused to conform to Shelley's radical ideas regarding religion and free love, ideas which would have understandably shocked, perhaps even horrified, a genteel young lady in 1810. Grove was, indeed, shocked and horrified, and promptly ended her romance with Shelley.

However, Shelley was already turning his attentions to a new potential convert, another chance to create the perfect woman, a schoolmate of his sisters named Harriet Westbrook. When they met, in January of 1811, Shelley was interested enough to have a copy of his gothic novel, St. Irvyne, sent to her, and to suggest that they "*correspond on matters philosophical and political*" (Cameron 89). Shelley came to know the Westbrooks well during the next months, for on April 24 he wrote to Hogg that Westbrook had "*gone to her prison-house*"--the boarding school--and that she was "*amiable, charitable and good.*" Shelley goes on to question his deepening interest in Westbrook, his need to mold her into a perfect being, going so far as to state that

> *it is, perhaps, scarcely doing her a kindness--it is, perhaps, inducing positive unhappiness--to point out to her a road which leads to perfection, the attainment of which, perhaps, does not repay the difficulties of the progress. What do you think of this? If trains of thought, development of mental energies influence in any degree a future state; if this is even possible—if it stands on at all securer ground than mere hypothesis; then is it not a service? Where am I gotten? perhaps into another ridiculous argument* (Ingpen 1: 57-58).

This letter is relevant for two reasons: first, we have Shelley's statement on perfection. At the age of 18, Shelley makes his first pronouncement that it is, indeed, perfection that he is seeking. Though he does question whether the actual "*attainment*" of perfection is truly worth the price one must pay in order to achieve it, equally relevant is the fact that Shelley brushes aside the potential for argument from, and with, Hogg on the matter. This quick dismissal of the subject suggests, at least to this reader, that Shelley was not willing to compromise, even a little, his belief in the possibility of perfection. In this regard, Shelley practices the attestation made in his revolutionary works that commitment to one's beliefs is of the utmost importance, perhaps the most important commitment one can make.

The second point of relevance in that letter of April 24 is its establishment of Westbrook as a 'cause' for Shelley, as well as another chance to create the perfect mate. By the time he composed the April 24 letter, Westbrook and Shelley had indulged in discourse enough so that she would have been well aware of his views, including those on parental tyranny and oppression (which he felt he had recently suffered from over the expulsion). Knowing those views, and how passionate Shelley could become when roused, Westbrook appealed to him for assistance in freeing her from her "*prison-house*," the boarding school where her father had sent her, where she was "*ostracized by the other pupils for being the friend of the 'atheist' Shelley*" (Cameron 91). Shelley explained to Hogg, from Rhayader, at the beginning of August that Westbrook had asked Shelley's advice in dealing with the situation, that he had advised resistance to her father, that Westbrook found that advice impossible to follow, but that she would run away with him, and thus had thrown herself upon Shelley's guardianship (Ingpen 1: 129-130).

So it was that Shelley found himself with Westbrook; the only solution, in the end, was for the two of them to elope. On August 25 they did just that, arriving in Edinburgh on the 28th; the next day, they were husband and wife. Perhaps Shelley, who had spoken out against the institution of marriage,[4] felt responsible for Westbrook's unhappiness, given that her relationship with him had caused her to be an outcast, and therefore felt it his duty to free her from that oppressive situation. Perhaps because she had followed his advice to "*resist*" her father's dictates--impossible for a teenage girl in 1811--he felt a sense of duty. Either way, his convictions against tyranny, whether from fathers or from kings, led him to compromise his views on marriage.

Shelley, however, did find what he considered, at least in the beginning, a companionable partner in Westbrook, for he wrote to Godwin on February 24, 1812 that his wife "*is a woman whose pursuits, hopes, fears, and sorrows were so similar to my own, that we married a few months ago*" (Ingpen 1: 265). Such was not always the case, though, for at the beginning of their relationship she had tried to argue against Shelley's beliefs, her fear of divine condemnation so great that she was even afraid to listen to his arguments. However, Shelley's powers of persuasion were greater than her fear, and he eventually won her over, freeing her soul, she declared, from the "*shackle[s of] such idle fears*" (Hawkins 55). Westbrook, then, was just what Shelley wanted: a young mind willing and capable of conforming to his beliefs and ideas, a young woman willing to put herself in his hands to be shaped and recreated into his conception of the ideal, perfect companion.

At the same time that he was getting to know Westbrook, Shelley met Elizabeth Hitchener, a schoolteacher ten years his senior, "*with whom he opened a correspondence on political and religious matters*" (Cameron 92). During the course of their correspondence, Shelley came to think of her as more than just a good friend; she became more important to him than merely an "*initiate.*" Hitchener came to be regarded almost as an extension of Shelley himself, one whose ideas and ideals he was able to conform to his own. In his letters to her he alternately called her "*Sister of my soul*" (Ingpen 1: 144, 145); "*my dearest friend*" (Ingpen 1: 213, 237, 267, 306); "*my friend, my dearest friend, the partner of my thoughts*" (Ingpen 1: 225); and, "*Friend of my soul*" (Ingpen 1: 303). In the early days of their friendship, Shelley questioned her religious beliefs and did his best to convince her that her beliefs were wrong, that his were right, and that she should therefore come around to his way of thinking. Just as he had persuaded Westbrook, Shelley's arguments eventually won over Hitchener. She became so important to Shelley that he confided to her on November 20, 1811: "*Writing is slow, soulless, incommunicative. I long to talk with you; my soul is bursting. Ideas, millions of ideas are crowding into it: it pants for communion with you*" (Ingpen 1: 166).

Hitchener was important, for she filled part of the void the estrangement from his parents and sisters had caused; Hitchener, a relatively new acquaintance, professed to support Shelley in both his marriage and in his political activities. She gave him the understanding his father couldn't give him, and Shelley responded in typical fashion by declaring his (Platonic) love for her. She was someone not only willing to listen to his arguments and statements, but someone who was willing to convert to them. She provided Shelley with understanding and sympathy, vital components to every relationship in Shelley's life. Shelley created an ideal being in his mind, a being based solely on Hitchener's correspondence, and obviously felt the need to have her near him, as a member of his new family. Finally, Shelley proposed that Hitchener come and live with him, Westbrook and her elder sister, Eliza, who were all residing together at Keswick. Hitchener would be their sister, and would share their lives and his plans for establishing equality in Ireland.

When Hitchener finally did come, and Shelley had four months to spend with the person, rather than the ideal he had created, getting to know her for who and what she really was, it was a less than ideal situation. Hitchener, much older than the newlyweds, was headstrong, and did her best to appropriate Eliza's role as unofficial head of the household; it was Eliza who controlled the finances and such matters as meal planning and preparation, and Hitchener wanted to be the one in charge of her "brother's" affairs. The situation finally came to a head, Westbrook and Eliza frustrated and angered at Hitchener's attempted takeover, and Shelley had to step in and ask her to leave; she agreed only after getting Shelley to promise her an annual allowance of £100. Without it, she threatened to go to the authorities and disclose Shelley's plans for Irish assistance. Needless to say, the Shelleys were relieved to be rid of her, and after her departure, Westbrook wrote to a friend that

> *we were entirely deceived in her character as to her republicanism, and in short everything else which she pretended to be. We were not long in finding out our great disappointment in her.... She built all her hopes on being able to separate me from my dearly loved Percy, and had the artfulness to say that Percy was really in love with her.... He thought her sensible but nothing more.... It was a long time ere*

THE QUEST FOR PERFECTION

> *we could possibly get her away, till at last Percy said he would give her £100 per annum.*

(Ingpen 1:365)

Both husband and wife disregarded the fact that Shelley had encouraged Hitchener, and, in a letter to Hogg dated December 3, 1812, Shelley echoed his wife's sentiments:

> *The Brown Demon, as we call our late tormentor and schoolmistress, must receive her stipend [the £100]. I pay it with a heavy heart and an unwilling hand; but it must be so. . . . Certainly she is embarrassed and poor, and we being in some degree the cause, we ought to obviate it. She is an artful, superficial, ugly, hermaphroditical beast of a woman, and my astonishment at my fatuity, inconsistency, and bad taste was never so great, as after living four months with her as an inmate. What would Hell be, were such a woman in Heaven?* (Ingpen 1:367)

Shelley vented his hurt and anger in a typical manner, attacking Hitchener with his pen, writing offensive words to a third party. Intriguingly, Shelley now viewed the former "*sister of [his] soul*" as an unattractive, insincere, deceitful, and bisexual "*beast.*" In his anger, he had stripped her of her femininity, and her goodness, and turned her into a sexually indiscernible, and evil, creature. Shelley learned the hard way from this incident that the reality rarely lives up to the ideal. Through their correspondence, Shelley had come to think of Hitchener as the perfect female, as the "*sister of [his] soul*," that was the image created on paper. He soon came to realize that she was really nothing more than a mere mortal woman, perhaps, as Westbrook said, hoping to snare a Baronet's son for herself; were this the case, and she proved to be only interested in position and wealth, then Shelley would have been especially stung by her reality. In any event, this was only one of many times that Shelley would become bitterly hurt and disappointed when a real person shattered his ideal of them.

By March of 1814, there was growing discontent in the Shelley marriage, so much so that Shelley moved out of their house for a while, staying with his friends, the Boinvilles. When Hogg visited Shelley there that month, he noticed some strange behavior, such as Shelley's use of wooden washtubs for small boats. Such behavior caused Hogg to fear for his friend's mental well-being, a justified concern, for Holmes concludes that "*Shelley was on the verge of breakdown*" (224). On March 16, Shelley wrote Hogg a letter which probably did little to ease his friend's mind, a desperate and rambling letter, in which he proclaimed that the Boinville home was his new home, where he had been given the "*support and consolation*" that had been lacking in his marriage. He then went on to declare his intense hatred of Eliza Westbrook, who had begun to come between the young husband and wife. More than anything, though, Shelley feared her influence and control over his baby, Ianthe, the only person he felt he could now turn to for "*consolation of sympathy*" (Ingpen 1: 417-419). One may deduce from this letter that the 'real world' had become too much for Shelley. Unable to cope with the reality of his life, he fled to the Boinvilles' home, which became the ideal environment, a place Shelley described as a "*paradise which has nothing of mortality*" (Ingpen 1:418).

THE QUEST FOR PERFECTION

The real problem, however, was Eliza: his sister-in-law was an emotional and financial burden, and his wife was apparently too much under her sister's influence to understand that Shelley desired and needed time and space alone with his new family--Westbrook had given birth to a daughter, Eliza Ianthe, on June 23, 1813. Especially after the Hitchener visit, and its disastrous results, Shelley most likely craved a sense that all was once more right in his world. Not helping matters much was Mr. Westbrook's demand that a second marriage take place,

> *to remove possible legal irregularities from the Scottish marriage of 1811 . . . [and] to have his daughter's legal position in relation to Shelley's inheritance made absolutely certain, especially since the emotional position was steadily deteriorating for all to see.*
> (Holmes 226)

Shelley was no longer receiving from Westbrook the compassion, understanding, and sympathy he craved, though he relented to Mr. Westbrook's demand, probably to prevent any more tension and discord in his life, as well as to secure his daughter's legal position. The second ceremony occurred less than one week after Shelley's March 16 letter to Hogg; emphasizing the breakdown of the relationship, Shelley was back at the Boinville home by the end of March, while Westbrook left for a holiday with the baby and Eliza. There, "*Shelley moved in a dream world, totally disillusioned with Harriet's love, but desperately seeking some alternative relationship*" (Holmes 227).

When financial matters forced Shelley to stay in London that June, he would find that "*alternative relationship*" with Mary Wollstonecraft Godwin. Shelley was struck by the pretty and intelligent teenager from the moment he first saw her; as we have already stated, Shelley considered her to be the natural and perfect partner for one such as himself. His friend Thomas Love Peacock recalled a conversation he had with Shelley soon after he had first met Wollstonecraft Godwin:

> *... calmly he said: 'Every one who knows me must know that the partner of my life should be one who can feel poetry and understand philosophy. Harriet is a noble animal, but she can do neither'. I said: 'It always appeared to me that you were very fond of Harriet'. Without affirming or denying this, he answered: 'But you did not know how I hated her sister'.* (Peacock 336)

Once the relationship with Westbrook was all but over, and once she had ceased to be his ideal--slipping, as she did, from his control into her sister's control--Shelley began to replace her with the next "*potential initiate*," seeking in another the qualities which Westbrook lacked. The daughter of Godwin and Wollstonecraft, by virtue of her heritage and upbringing, seemed capable of feeling poetry and understanding philosophy. To Shelley, she was perfect, and he eventually eloped with her, leaving his first wife behind, following an already-established pattern of discarding people once they ceased to fill his requirements and live up to his ideal.

However, Shelley did not want to abandon Westbrook altogether, for he still felt some degree of concern for her, and invited Westbrook to live with them, in a letter echoing his earlier invitation to Hitchener, as his and

Wollstonecraft Godwin's sister. No longer Shelley's perfect companion, his ideal mate, and his sexual partner, she could now become the platonic member of his new family. Wollstonecraft Godwin would now be the perfect companion and ideal mate, as well as the sexual partner, meaning Westbrook would have to watch another woman take her place in her husband's life. It was a role Westbrook refused to accept, and, heartbroken and shocked, she promptly refused. Shelley accepted her answer, leaving her to face the world alone as an abandoned wife. In November 1816, Westbrook ended her pain, suffering, and humiliation by drowning herself in the Thames. Shelley and Wollstonecraft Godwin married on December 16, 1816.

In the six years following their elopement (1814-1820), Shelley and his second wife shared many happy hours together; most of the time, she seemed to live up to his idealistic expectations, providing him with the support, compassion, and understanding that were essential to him as both a man and as a poet. However, they also suffered their share of tragedies, foremost among them the deaths of three children (a newborn in 1815, Clara in 1818 and William in 1819), tragedies which would instigate the onset of Shelley's disillusionment with Godwin Shelley. The deaths of her babies were understandably devastating to Godwin Shelley, who suffered nervous breakdowns each time and withdrew into herself so far that no one could reach her. Husband and wife drifted emotionally apart during these times, Shelley not giving Godwin Shelley the understanding and support she needed, and Godwin Shelley not giving him the encouragement and understanding he needed. In November of 1819, though, another son was born, named for his father and the city of his conception: Percy Florence. This child consoled Godwin Shelley, yet, at the same time, filled her with fear and dread that he, too, would die. Godwin Shelley, it seems, never recovered completely from these losses, something which Shelley could never really understand. This is not to say that Shelley was not saddened by the deaths of his children, for he was deeply saddened; however, Shelley regarded death as a natural part of life, indeed, as we shall see, as the achievement of ultimate perfection. Thus, the Shelleys' closeness suffered as a result. It would appear that Shelley's ideal mate was only human, after all, a fact which left him feeling abandoned, as evidenced by stanzas dedicated to her and found among his papers for 1819, one of which says:

> *My dearest Mary, wherefore hast thou gone,*
>
> *And left me in this dreary world alone?*
>
> *Thy form is here indeed--a lovely one--*
>
> *But thou art fled, gone down the weary road,*
>
> *That leads to Sorrow's most obscure abode;*
>
> *Thou sittest on the hearth of pale despair,*
>
> *Where*
>
> *For thine own sake I cannot follow thee.*
>
> (Shelley 577)

These lines reveal Shelley's frustration and feeling of abandonment, as well as his belief that the cares and burdens of the real world lead to unhappiness and imperfection. Throughout the next year, the gulf between Shelley and

THE QUEST FOR PERFECTION

Godwin Shelley remained, at least to the point that they both turned to their friends, old and new alike, for stimulus and support. Mary found joy in Prince Alexander Mavrocordato, a Greek exile with whom, according to Godwin Shelley's journal, she frequently visited (Jones 141ff). If Godwin Shelley "*delighted*" (White 385) in her new friend, Shelley was even more taken by another new acquaintance which was to enter their lives.

While the Shelleys were residing at Pisa they made the acquaintance of Professor Pacciani; on November 20, 1820 Pacciani took Godwin Shelley and her half-sister Claire Clairmont to the Convent of St. Anna, where he introduced them to Teresa Emilia Viviani. Teresa, or Emilia as the Shelleys called her, was then 19 years old, and had been "*imprisoned*" at the convent for three years when she came into the Shelleys' lives (White 387). When Shelley himself first met her that December, he was instantly drawn to her; his cousin, Thomas Medwin, had accompanied Shelley, and would recall that first visit and their first impressions of Viviani:

> *Emilia was indeed lovely and interesting. Her profuse black hair, tied in the most simple knot, after the manner of a Greek Muse in the Florence Gallery, displayed to its full height her brow, fair as that of the marble of which I speak. She was also of about the same height as the antique. Her features possessed a rare faultlessness, and almost Grecian contour, the nose and forehead making a straight line. . . .*
> (Holmes 625)

Viviani, then, in Shelley's eyes, was as close to physical perfection as one could hope to find in this mortal world. As students of Shelley's life know, he spent many hours in the museums of Italy, studying and gaining inspiration from the Greek artifacts contained within them. Shelley transferred the physical perfection of those Greek statues onto Viviani, who, while indeed beautiful, became a vision of physical perfection in his eyes. We know, too, that Viviani was a highly intelligent and sensitive young woman, who wrote poetry and essays. One is reminded of Shelley's description of the ideal mate: that she should "*feel poetry and understand philosophy*," words first spoken in reference to Godwin Shelley. Viviani, it seems, was beginning to take the place formerly held in Shelley's affections by Godwin Shelley; when his wife proved too human, and not perfect, Shelley began looking for his next initiate. It was into this situation that Viviani entered, and, to Shelley, she must have appeared to be a dream come true.

Shelley was not only struck by Viviani's beauty and intellect, however; echoing many past relationships with females, especially Westbrook, Shelley came to regard Viviani almost as a cause. He formed attractions with young women who were prisoners of parental tyranny, and always wanted to take it upon himself to free them, and ultimately control and recreate them. Viviani was forced to stay in the convent while her father, an influential Governor, found a suitable husband for her, though her situation was really no different from that of any well-bred Italian girl of the early nineteenth century. However, when she informed Shelley that she did not want to be there, and that she did not particularly want to be consigned to an arranged marriage, the revolutionary in

Shelley once more surfaced. He hoped to use the few connections he had made in Italy to help free Viviani from the convent, but his letters of appeal were ultimately of no help.

Viviani was not just a vision of Intellectual Beauty to Shelley, nor was she merely another cause; Emilia Viviani gave Shelley what no one else had given him--complete sympathy, something he had been given by each of his perfect women, but which had ceased once the ideal had faded. Viviani instantly recognized in Shelley the tormented Poet, the being searching for complete fulfillment, understanding and companionship. Viviani, then, saw Shelley for what he really was, a man and a poet forever becoming dissatisfied with, and disillusioned by, the people in his life. However, she never discouraged his attentions, nor tried to end his idealization of her, though, it must be noted, she never encouraged the union Shelley would envision in his poetry. Viviani, in fact, seems to have idealized Shelley, turning him into a misunderstood and ethereal being. Only two weeks after meeting Shelley, Viviani wrote to Godwin Shelley on December 14, 1820, describing her feelings for Shelley:

> *His many misfortunes, his unjust persecutions, and his firm and innate virtue in the midst of these terrible and unmerited sorrows filled my heart with admiration and affection and made me think, and perhaps not untruly, that he is not a human creature; he has only a human exterior, but the interior is all divine.*

(White 389)

However rhapsodic Viviani's tribute may sound, her feelings about the Shelleys should not be misunderstood. She regarded Percy, Mary and Claire as her surrogate family, and in her letters to Shelley she referred to him as her dear brother; indeed, Shelley "*realized that her affection for him was genuinely that of a sister*" (White 389). As Newman Ivey White explains, Shelley believed that a poet really consisted of two separate identities, the poet and the man. The man Shelley realized that it was impossible to have any other relationship with Viviani; his rationale told him that they could never fulfill the spiritual marriage the poet longed for (White 427). To the poet, Viviani represented everything he had been searching for his entire adult life--companionship with, and understanding and sympathy from, one who seemed to be an extension of himself. The relationship the man and the real Viviani shared was that of friendship; the relationship the poet had with the Viviani who was the embodiment of his ideal was a "*close spiritual kinship*" (White 391), a relationship Shelley had sought in each of his perfect women.

In December 1820, Shelley began his long poem about Viviani, a poem which has caused at least one Shelley scholar to question how Emily, as he calls her in the poem, could be "*A Metaphor of Spring and Youth and Morning*" (line 120). After all, this scholar reasoned, Emily is a human being, and human beings cannot be metaphors. There is a reason why the Emily of the poem is a metaphor, a reason which originates in Shelley's adolescence: his need to idealize people.

Since Shelley considered Viviani to be an extension of himself, a part of his essential being, the poet titled his work Epipsychidion, a Greek word meaning "*soul out of my soul*" (line 238). This poem chronicles not only Shelley's spiritual relationship with Viviani, but his quest to find, in human form, the embodiment of all that is pure, divine and good. During the time in which he knew Viviani, Shelley was coming to realize that "*complete companionship is possible only within one's own thoughts*" (White 92), that the perfect human relationship was with one's own soul. To the poet Shelley, Viviani was a part of his soul, another being made from that soul. Therefore, their relationship was the ideal, perfect relationship.

Shelley's poem opens with lines exalting the spiritual qualities of Emily. He alternately refers to her as "*Sweet Spirit!*" (line 1), "*High, spirit-wingèd Heart!*" (line 13), and "*Seraph of Heaven!*" (line 21). Stanza five opens with the revealing lines, "*I never thought before my death to see / youth's vision thus made perfect*" (lines 41-42), lines which reveal his belief that perfection will be revealed and obtained only in death. Shelley also implies that he no longer expected to find his "*vision*," his perfect woman, in human form, that the dream woman had fled from him too many times for him to expect her to appear on this earth in all her beauty and perfection. These lines lead one to inquire whether, upon his disillusionment with Godwin Shelley, he had not begun to doubt the existence, in human form, of his perfect woman. Shelley closes the stanza by stating that "*I am not thine: I am part of thee*," a line which echoes the poem's title. In the opening stanzas of his poem, then, Shelley establishes Emily as a being more than merely human, and himself as part of that being. They are spirits both "*too gentle to be human*" (line 21), whose love is truly divine and Platonic.

The anonymous reader is directly addressed in stanza seven, and is told the love story of the Poet and Emily. She frees him from this life, luring him "*towards sweet Death,*" leading him "*into light, life, peace*" (lines 73-74). Once more, Shelley reiterates his belief that true perfection comes only in death. Just as a dream provides an escape for the mind, so did Emily provide the Poet with a means of escape; indeed, she was Shelley's living dream. The analogy is taken one step further when he describes her, in terms reminiscent of his early poem about Grove, as one connected to Nature and celestial bodies (lines 75-111). This passage is important, for in it Shelley imbues Emily with many of the qualities and attributes of Nature, the seat of perfection upon this earth. She is, therefore, no longer merely human--she is a perfect being, a child of Nature who has inherited the grace, beauty, and perfection that Nature alone can bestow. Just as Spring awakens the earth after Winter, and brings new life, beauty and intoxicating fragrances to the world, Emily awakens the Poet from a cold, winter-like sleep, bringing to him the life, warmth, beauty and intoxication of Spring, as well as the perfection that is now hers, and which he will, in turn, acquire. Emily is, in this passage, made part of Nature. The implication is that, if she and the Poet are part of the same being, then they are both, in essence, children of that "*Great Parent*" (Alastor, line 45), Nature.

Shelley enforces Emily's dehumanization by stating that she is

a mortal shape indued

With love and life and light and deity,

And motion which may change but cannot die;

An image of some bright Eternity;

THE QUEST FOR PERFECTION

A shadow of some golden dream; a Splendour

Leaving the third sphere pilotless; a tender

Reflection of the eternal Moon of Love

Under whose motions life's dull billows move;

A Metaphor of Spring and Youth and Morning;

A Vision like incarnate April, warning,

With smiles and tears, Frost the Anatomy

Into his summer grave. (112-123)

These lines tell us with certainty that Emily is no longer human; she is "*a mortal shape*," an "*image*," a "*shadow*," a "*tender reflection*," and a "*vision*" which "*cannot die*," which is immortal. She is, he says, his "*golden dream*" come to life. It is interesting to note here that for Shelley, the ultimate relationship was that between man and Nature.

This relationship, as we shall see, was the perfect relationship; it was the purest, truest, and most spiritual relationship man could ever experience. Nature alone was perfect in this world; it was Shelley's desire to help make man, society and all creation as perfect as Nature. No mere mortal, no human being, therefore, could satisfy and fulfill his desires, needs and wants, for human beings are not perfect. Emilia offered Shelley complete sympathy and understanding, and this made her, to the poet Shelley, an extension of himself, a part of his own soul, his epipsyche. In order for them to have the perfect relationship, Emilia could not remain a mere mortal. She ceased to be Emilia the human being, then, and became instead Emily the ideal; as such, Shelley became her creator, imposing upon her all that is best, beautiful, pure, immortal, and perfect. As Shelley states, "*In many mortal forms I rashly sought / the shadow of that idol of my thought*" (lines 167-168); he realized, then, that a mortal being could never truly be his ideal mate. Thus, the Emilia who was imprisoned within the convent became Emily, the "*Spouse! Sister! Angel! . . . in the fields of Immortality . . . a divine presence in a place divine*" (lines 130, 133, 135).

Shelley, the man, was unable to free Emilia from her prison and her fate, marriage, "*which is,*" he said, "*the same as being dead*" (White 430). Shelley, the poet, however, was able to fulfill his fantasy within the lines of his poem. The Poet rescues Emily from her convent prison and together they sail away by ship to the perfect place, to Paradise, where no beings but them reside. Interestingly, all that the Poet brings with him from the world of man are "*books and music*" (line 519), which Shelley was constantly surrounded by himself. Their Paradise, their Elysian universe, "*is a favoured place, [where] famine or blight, / pestilence, war and earthquake, never light / upon its mountain-peaks*" (lines 461-463). He owns this place-- "*this isle and house are mine*" (line 513)--and so has banished all that Shelley the revolutionary found ugly, cruel, and mean in the world. In his poem, at least, Shelley has created the perfect world and the perfect partner. The Poet tells Emily that they will grow old there together, that they shall share "*one life, one death, / one Heaven, one Hell, one immortality, / and one annihilation*" (lines 585-587), and that upon their death will become enjoined with Nature. They will thus form a trinity, three beings dwelling within one soul: the Poet, Emily, and Nature; Brother, Sister, and Mother united for eternity. In

THE QUEST FOR PERFECTION

their deaths, they will become divine, like Shelley's Nature, beings which will be pure, good, and free of sin. Like the first, perfect, man and woman--Adam and Eve--they shall reside in the perfect place, a Garden of Eden, where there will be no cruelty, suffering, hunger, nor pain. In his poem, if not in reality, they shall have complete, true perfection.

Shelley closes his poem with an exhortation to the poem itself to "*go, kneel at your Sovereign's feet*" (line 592). He commands the verses to tell Emily that

love's very pain is sweet,

But its reward is in the world divine

Which if not here, it builds beyond the grave.

So shall ye live when I am there. (596-599)

Shelley has come to realize that Paradise is reached only in death, just as the ultimate truths concerning life, death, existence, and life after death are revealed to one after death. Just as the man realized that a relationship with Emilia was impossible, and that his truly ideal mate did not exist in mortal form, the poet realized that he could experience that relationship, that plane of perfection, only within the lines of his own poem. Shelley became disillusioned with Emilia when he realized that she had finally agreed to the arranged marriage to Luigi Biondi, the man her father had picked for her (White 426). As he would write to a friend on June 18, 1822, Epipsychidion

> *is an idealized history of my life and feelings. I think one is always in love with something or other; the error, and I confess it is not easy for spirits cased in flesh and*

> *blood to avoid it, consists in seeking in a mortal image the likeness of what is perhaps eternal.*

(Ingpen 2: 976)

In other words, Vivani was a human being rather than an ideal, a fact Shelley was unable to come to terms with. Upon her marriage, as Shelley's note to the poem shows, he distanced himself from the part of him that had composed the poem; indeed, he goes so far as to declare that

> *the Writer of the following Lines died at Florence, as he was preparing for a voyage to one of the wildest of the Sporades, which he had bought, and where he had fitted up the ruins of an old building, and where it was his hope to have raised a scheme of life, suited perhaps to that happier and better world of which he is now an inhabitant, but hardly practicable in this. His life was singular, less on account of the romantic vicissitudes which diversified it, than the ideal tinge which it received from his own character and feelings.*
> (Shelley 406)

The part of Shelley which had composed Epipsychidion was dead, unable to continue life in this world, and Shelley, realizing this, consigned him to Paradise. Perhaps, too, Shelley had become discontent with his search for the perfect woman.

His writings reveal that he had begun to realize that perfect people do not exist, at least not in the mortal world of mankind, and that it was a hopeless and painful task to continue the search. Perhaps these statements of Shelley's help explain why he turned to poetry--the embodiment and seat of Intellectual Beauty--rather than a mortal form, as he continued his quest for the ideal. Unable to control human beings as he felt obsessed to do, he turned his attentions to something he could completely control: his writing.

IV: Poet and Prophet: Shelley and Poetry

Realizing the impossibility of completely controlling and recreating another human being, Shelley turned to poetry in his continued search for perfection. His poetry was something he could directly and entirely control, something he could truly create and shape into whatever he desired. Shelley felt that poets were supreme beings, closer to the seat of perfection--Nature--than were other human beings, and that, as such, their productions had the potential to be perfect. Through his work, Shelley not only hoped to effect the revolution he desired, but also he hoped to achieve artistic perfection.

In February and March of 1821, after he finished Epipsychidion, Shelley began work on an essay he titled A Defense of Poetry. In this essay, he explores the meaning and function of poetry and the poet, his definitions containing "*the very essence of his life and thought*" (White 403). Not surprisingly, Shelley states that Poets are set apart from other men by virtue of their ability to look into the hearts, minds, and souls of men, as if with a jeweler's eye, to record what is found there. The Poet is, therefore, a supreme being.

The Poet also possesses the ability, indeed, the duty, to show his fellow beings not only the truth of the present but the possibility of the future; poetry thus becomes a force guiding mankind toward eternal truth and beauty. The Poet's thoughts and words are the seeds which will give birth, in the future, to the ideal vision of the Poet, making mankind and his world perfect, "*redeem[ing] from decay the visitations of the divinity in man*" (Reiman, Poetry and Prose 505), bringing mankind back to his perfect origins. The Poet should be a champion of the people, desiring to "*awaken [them] to work a beneficial change in opinion or institution*" (Reiman, Poetry and Prose 508), using his poetry to inspire and effect that change, and bring perfection into reality.

Shelley's essay turns from the public role of the Poet to the personal life of the Poet, giving an intriguing insight into Shelley's desire for perfection. Shelley says that the Poet, as an example to the people, "*ought personally to be the happiest, the best, the wisest, and the most illustrious of men*" (Reiman, Poetry and Prose 506). What Shelley has described is a person whose life is without any personal cares, concerns, or worries, without any sadness, and without any faults. If the Poet is not allowed to have any concerns or sadness, if he is supposed to be forever carefree, happy, and faultless, then he is not really human. After all, to be human is to suffer and to err. Shelley has yet again denied the existence of evil, turning the Poet into an ideal, perfect being. In light of this statement, one comes to better understand Shelley's inability to face the everyday concerns which befall every human being, and his obsessive need to be enveloped by a carefree, perfect environment.

Given the path that Shelley followed in life, becoming a poet and "*prophet*" of the world, it is clear that, from an early age, Shelley felt he "*had a paramount mission*" (White 403) to accomplish, and that the best method for him to do so would be through poetry. As he told Godwin in a letter dated January 10, 1812, he

THE QUEST FOR PERFECTION

> *beheld, in short, that [he] had duties to perform....*
> *[He could not descend to common life: the sublime*
> *interest of poetry, lofty and exalted achievements, the*
> *proselytism of the world, the equalization of its*
> *inhabitants, were to [him] the soul of [his] soul.*
> (Ingpen 1: 219-220)

Later that year, on August 18, he would supplement these thoughts by stating that, for the purpose of expressing one's "*constitutional enthusiasm . . . a poem is safe: the iron-souled Attorney-General would scarcely dare to attack [it]*" (Ingpen 1: 358). These thoughts were, of course, voiced before Shelley had written the controversial and dangerous Laon and Cythna, and before his dangerous political writings in Ireland. In 1812, Shelley believed that poetry was the perfect vehicle through which to initiate and execute the reformations he envisioned.

The thoughts expressed in these early letters, and in A Defense of Poetry, were the very thoughts and ideas which Shelley expressed in his most powerful poetry, principally the "Ode to the West Wind," where he clearly states that the Poet's mission is to instigate the revolution--with Nature's assistance--that will, in turn, bring into existence the perfect world.

V: The Ideal Relationship: The Poet and Nature

In his childhood, Shelley began to explore the relationship between man and Nature. As he matured, Shelley came to idealize Nature, creating the perfect Nature in both his imagination and his works. Shelley acknowledged the divine power of Nature to recreate itself each spring, but he denied its dark side, refusing to accept that cruelty and death--animals killing other animals for survival or territorial disputes, for example--are inherent components of Nature. To Shelley, Nature remained the seat of perfection, the place where man's journey toward perfection begins.

Shelley's first mature poem, Queen Mab, is the first of his works to deal seriously with the search for perfection. In the poem, the heroine, Ianthe, is taken, while asleep, by Mab, the Queen of the Fairies, to Heaven, where her soul can view earth. From her vantage point, Ianthe is able to see both the good and (especially) the bad of the world, and, by viewing the revolutions of the past, present, and future, is given a vision of how to create and maintain a perfect world. This is, undeniably, Shelley's most optimistic poem, the unabashed optimism due no doubt to his young age and relative inexperience in the world. Shelley was only 20 when he composed Queen Mab in the autumn and winter of 1812-1813, and was an idealistic revolutionary, a young man who yearned to make the world of the early nineteenth century the perfect world of Ianthe's vision. He still thought it possible for one man standing alone against the world, against the powers that be, to affect the peaceful, bloodless revolution and subsequent changes that would give birth to that Elysian world. The poem was first conceived by Shelley on December 10, 1811, when he was living in Keswick; the following day he wrote to Elizabeth Hitchener that he was planning a poem which he "*intend[ed] to be by anticipation a picture of the manners, simplicity, and delights of a perfect state of society, tho' still earthly.*" In his self-assured manner, he went on to say that he would "*accomplish it, and publish,*" and that he would next "*draw a picture of Heaven*" (Ingpen 1:192). Shelley's idealism is clearly evident in this letter; so too is his desire for a state of perfection.

To Shelley, that perfection was not to be found in man, nor in any of his earthly creations; rather, true perfection was to be found only in Nature, the creation of a perfect Deity. As he says in Queen Mab, Nature alone is pure and perfect; mankind is not. Man must realize that Nature had not made it, as a race, so vile and capable of cruelty; man itself, through all its centuries of evolution-- supposedly to the highest and noblest of life forms--turned itself into the mean creatures--the "*Kings, priests, and statesmen*" (line 104), the corrupted, the murderers of man and beast alike--Shelley writes out against. Mankind had fallen prey to Satan's tempting promises of wealth and power, and had turned greedy, selfish, and cruel as a result. The man who had once been close to Nature, who was pure, who had lived in the Garden of Eden, who did not have the blood of innocent humans and beasts on his hands, was long gone; however, Shelley's desire was to revive this man, in order that it would replace the cruel, greedy, revengeful man that had come into existence. As he says in the poem,

THE QUEST FOR PERFECTION

Hath Nature's soul . . .

filled the meanest worm that crawls in dust

With spirit, thought, and love; on Man alone,

Partial in causeless malice, wantonly

Heaped ruin, vice and slavery; his soul

Blasted with withering curses. . . .

Nature!--no!

Kings, priests, and statesmen, blast the human flower

Even in its tender bud; their influence darts

Like subtle poison through the bloodless veins

Of desolate society. The child,

Ere he can lisp his mother's sacred name,

Swells with the unnatural pride of crime, and lifts

His baby-sword even in a hero's mood.

. . . .

Let priest-led slaves cease to proclaim that man

Inherits vice and misery, when force

And falsehood hang even o'er the cradled babe,

Stifling with rudest grasp all natural good.

(89, 96-100, 104-111, 118-121)

In these lines, Shelley clearly places the blame for mankind's state upon its own conscience. Certain men in particular are to blame for mankind's current state: the rulers and leaders of government, church, and society. They have manipulated, controlled, and brainwashed the citizens of the world, leading their subjects further from Nature and closer to the materialistic world of man. These rulers have taught mankind, through example, to be filled with hate, cruelty, and revenge, rather than the love, kindness, and charity that had filled mankind at the beginning of human history. After centuries of oppression and domination, mankind was either unable or unwilling to break the tyrants' hold and influence on it. In Shelley's eyes, then, even the lowly worm is filled with more love and thought than is man; the reason is obvious: the worm has remained close to Nature, while man has turned away from it, to seek the power and the pleasures of the material world. This poem marks the beginning of Shelley's mission to free mankind from the evil influences of society's leaders, to reintroduce mankind to its "*great Mother*" (Alastor, line 2), and to thus make man a being free of all evil.

A variation of this idea is seen again, in a poem composed during the summer of 1815, when Shelley was residing at Bishopgate, Windsor Park. By this time, Shelley had been through one failed marriage, and his poetry suggests that he was then searching for the perfect relationship. In the course of this search, he consequently came to believe that the perfect relationship is that between man and Nature. "A Summer Evening Churchyard--Lechlade, Gloucestershire," was inspired by a ten-day boat trip on the Thames taken that August by Shelley, his friend Peacock, Wollstonecraft Godwin and her step-brother Charles Clairmont. During their two-night stay at Lechlade, Shelley wrote the poem, in which he says,

> *Thus solemnized and softened, death is mild*
>
> *And terrorless as this serenest night:*
>
> *Here could I hope, like some inquiring child*
>
> *Sporting on grave, that death did hide from human sight*
>
> *Sweet secrets, or beside its breathless sleep*
>
> *That loveliest dreams perpetual watch did keep.*

(25-30)

In these lines, lines directly inspired by Nature, Shelley hopes for the possibility that death holds "*sweet secrets*" of great import; relevant, too, is that he realizes and voices this hope while sitting in a churchyard, the resting place of the "*departed dead*" ("Beauty," line 52). This idea was to appear in many of Shelley's poems.

<u>Alastor; or, the Spirit of Solitude</u> was, as Godwin Shelley wrote in her note to the poem,

> *composed on his return. He spent his days under the oak-shades of Windsor Great Park; and the magnificent woodland was a fitting study to inspire the various descriptions of forest-scenery we find in the poem.... The death which he had often contemplated during the last months as certain and near he here represented....* (Shelley 31)

Death is again linked to Nature in Shelley's attempts to create perfection.

This poem, too, then, was inspired by Nature--the landscape seen and visited on his recent boat trip and the woods of Windsor Great Park. <u>Alastor</u>, it should be noted, opens with a Nature that is spiritualized. The Narrator--Shelley--immediately numbers himself among Nature's children, and proclaims his love for these siblings:

> *Earth, ocean, air, belovèd brotherhood!*
>
> *If our great Mother has imbued my soul*
>
> *With aught of natural piety to feel*
>
> *Your love, and recompense the boon with mine:*
>
> . . . .
>
> *If no bright bird, insect, or gentle beast*
>
> *I consciously have injured, but still loved*
>
> *And cherished these my kindred; then forgive*
>
> *This boast, belovèd brethren, and withdraw*
>
> *No portion of your wonted favour now!* (1-4; 13-17)

Interestingly, this "*solemn song*" (line 19) is addressed to the Narrator's "*brethren*"--elements and animals--and their "*great Mother*"--Nature--rather than to a human being, since the poem is, essentially, about the "*desperate longing for a transcending and paradisal form of love*" (Holmes, 247), a love that, in its perfection, is impossible to discover. One is led to inquire as to why the narrator considers himself a member of Nature's family, but never claims kinship with the human family. Some feasible reasons include Shelley's failed relationships: the loss of his first love, his cousin Harriet Grove; the estrangement from his (biological) family; the disillusionment caused by the "*sister of his soul*," correspondent Elizabeth Hitchener; and the dissolution of his first marriage, to Harriet Westbrook.

Add to this list the temporary breakup of his friendship with Thomas Jefferson Hogg over Hogg's supposed seduction of Westbrook, as well as the once-idolized William Godwin's growing demands for financial support from Shelley, and one has ample reason why Shelley would have begun questioning the true value and nature of human relationships. For instance, Shelley wrote to Godwin on March 16, 1816:

> *Do not talk of forgiveness again to me, for my blood boils in my veins, and my gall rises against all that bears the human form, when I think of what I, their benefactor and ardent lover, have endured of enmity and contempt from all mankind.*
> (Ingpen 1: 469)

These words of anger and pain clearly show how disillusioned the idealistic Shelley was becoming; one who was, in his own eyes, working for the betterment and perfectibility of man had been bitterly and sharply stung by the people he had pinned his greatest hopes and affections upon.

If the Narrator represents Shelley's thoughts and beliefs, so too does the Poet-Hero character. The Poet is a child of Nature, just as is the narrator. We are introduced to the Poet with the lines,

> *By solemn vision, and bright silver dream,*
>
> *His infancy was nurtured. Every sight*
>
> *And sound from the vast earth and ambient air,*
>
> *Sent to his heart its choicest impulses.* (67-70)

The Poet and the Narrator, both children of Nature, long to know the secrets which Nature holds, the ultimate secrets of life, of death, and even of life after death, or, as the Narrator says, "*the tale / of what we are*" (lines 27-28).

The two have sought these truths in different ways, though both employ methods that Shelley himself used both as a child and as an adult. The Narrator sought Nature's "*deep mysteries*" (line 23) by having

> *I have made my bed In charnels and on coffins, where black death*
>
> *Keeps record of the trophies won from thee,*
>
> *Hoping to still these obstinate questionings*
>
> *Of thee and thine, by forcing some lone ghost*
>
> *Thy messenger, to render up the tale*
>
> *Of what we are.* (23-28)

Note the similarity of these lines to those from "A Summer Evening Churchyard;" in both poems, Shelley is seeking answers from the dead who are entombed within the earth,

THE QUEST FOR PERFECTION

within Nature, and therefore possess that perfect relationship. Shelley believed that once one was dead and entombed within the earth--Nature--one was then able to absorb Nature's perfection. This perfection would remain with the dead throughout the soul's eternal existence, guiding the dead toward the answers he had been seeking in life, revealing the great mysteries and secrets of life, death, creation, and existence. The veil between life and death would be lifted, thus imparting all divine knowledge to the dead. For this reason, Shelley considered the relationship between man and Nature to be the perfect relationship, for it is through Nature that man is led to the seat of divine wisdom.

The Poet of Alastor, on the other hand, pursued this knowledge by studying ancient history and the philosophers of old. Unlike the Narrator, he turns to mankind for the answers, rather than to Nature. When the Poet leaves his idyllic home in Nature and ventures out into the world of man, his demise is imminent. The Poet has his first human contact with the Arab maiden (at least we may assume it is his first, since no others are mentioned) in the world of man. Before this contact, his had been "*innocent dreams*" (line 137), and he had been pure of thought. Once he experiences this contact, his innocence becomes corrupted, and

a vision on his sleep

There came, a dream of hopes that never yet

Had flushed his cheek. (158-160)

After he has the erotic dream of the vision, a vision of the ideal love that is described as being both human and Nature personified, and he sets out in search of this vision--the maiden--and abandons the search for the secrets of Nature, his landscape turns dark, dreary, and filled with death:

> *A gradual change was here,*
>
> *Yet ghastly. For, as fast years flow away,*
>
> *The smooth brow gathers, and the hair grows thin*
>
> *And white, and where irradiate dewy eyes*
>
> *Had shone, gleam stony orbs:--so from his steps*
>
> *Bright flowers departed, and the beautiful shade*
>
> *Of the green groves, with all their odorous winds*
>
> *And musical motions.* (532-539)

Nature seems to be mourning the Poet's decision to seek the perfect relationship with the maiden of his vision. Nature clothes itself in black--the black of evening and of death. For, not only is the Poet facing death at the end of the poem, but Nature, too, is dying: it projects "*tall spires of windlestrae*" (line 58) and "*grey rocks*" (line 527), and the stream is suddenly a "*struggling brook*" (line 528). The Poet is now in "*the lap of horror*" (line 578), a dark and imperfect Nature.

Noteworthy, though, is that when the Poet dies at the end "*he lay breathing there / at peace, and faintly smiling*" (lines 644-645). He has returned, in death, to a Nature of lush, green beauty, a perfect Nature.

Support for the Narrator's chosen path to enlightenment and the perfect relationship can be found in "Hymn to Intellectual Beauty," written in the summer of

THE QUEST FOR PERFECTION

1816. Godwin Shelley tells us that *"he spent the summer of the shore of the Lake of Geneva. The 'Hymn to Intellectual Beauty' was conceived during his voyage round the lake with Lord Byron"* (Shelley 532). In a letter to Peacock dated July 12, 1816, Shelley stated that their boat trip lasted eight days, and that the excursion was "*on every account delightful, but most especially, because then I first knew the divine beauty of Rousseau's imagination, as it exhibits itself in 'Julie'*" (Ingpen 2: 488-489). As he explained, the two poets made it a point to visit the scenes which made up the settings of the book.

Just as "A Summer Evening Churchyard" and <u>Alastor</u> were directly inspired by Nature, so, too, was the "Hymn." The Intellectual Beauty addressed in the title is, we see from the context of the poem, "*nonmaterial*;" that is, it is a "*shadow of some unseen Power*" (line 1), which is felt but remains "*yet dearer for its mystery*" (line 12). It is, then, a "*Spirit*" (line 13) not of this world.

In the autobiographical stanza V, Shelley writes of how, as a child, he had sought for the Truth, as do the Narrator and the Poet of <u>Alastor</u>:

> *While yet a boy I sought for ghosts, and sped*
>
> *Through many a listening chamber, cave and ruin,*
>
> *And starlight wood, with fearful steps pursuing*
>
> *Hopes of high talk with the departed dead.* (49-51)

These lines are remarkably similar to those from "A Summer Evening Churchyard" and the Narrator's words in <u>Alastor</u>, when he says, "*I have made my bed / in charnels and on coffins*" (lines 23-24), while

Like an inspired and desperate alchymist

Staking his very life on some dark hope,

Have I mixed awful talk and asking looks

With my most innocent love, until strange tears

Uniting with those breathless kisses made

Such magic as compels the charmèd night

To render up thy charge.... (29-37)

As a child, Shelley conducted many electrical experiments, read scientific books, and delighted in spending many hours in the cemetery of Warnham Church near the family home. There was a reason for these graveyard visits: Shelley desired to raise the dead so that he could inquire of them what death was really like, and, more importantly, what they had learned in death. This wish to commune with the dead remained with Shelley into his teenage years, as well; as Newman Ivey White explains,

> *he sought out the lore of magic and witchcraft, and learned incantations for raising ghosts and devils. At Field Place he planned to gain entrance to the charnel house at Warnham Church and watch beside the bones of the dead. Once at Eton he stole forth at midnight fearfully intent on raising a ghost; he repeated his incantation, drinking three times from a skull, and when no ghost appeared he concluded that the fault lay in his magic formula.* (18)

THE QUEST FOR PERFECTION

One may conclude that this preoccupation with the dead, rather than with the living, lies in the fact that Shelley truly believed that the dead, those with the closest relationship to Nature, could offer what no mere mortal being really could--the truth.

In light of these activities, Cronin's assessment of the vocabulary of stanzas V and VI as one that "*expresses a lack of contact with the normally human*" (227) is especially interesting. Shelley was, after all, calling upon the "*departed dead*," in the hope that they would reveal to him the mysteries of existence. Once more, the emphasis is on the poet's relationship with Nature (via the dead who are now part of it) rather than with a living human being.

In no other poem he had yet composed did Shelley explore the relationship between man and Nature as deeply as he does in "Mont Blanc," another work to spring from that summer of 1816, perhaps the most famous summer in literary history. Intriguingly, Godwin Shelley's story of creation and divine knowledge--<u>Frankenstein</u>--was conceived that summer. Shelley was particularly prolific that summer, conceiving and composing quite a number of works, poems which all pursue to some degree the most perfect of all relationships: that between man and Nature. Interestingly, these poems were each inspired by Nature, and "Mont Blanc" is no exception. In her notes to the poems of 1816, Godwin Shelley tells us that the poem was inspired by Shelley's view of the mountain as he journeyed through the Valley of Chamouni. Shelley himself was overcome with emotion, his soul overwhelmed at the sight of the mountain (Shelley 532).

In his significant biography of the poet, Newman Ivey White states that the two sides of Shelley--the scientific and the poetic--were both excited by the glaciers he had seen that July 23. The logical, scientific part of Shelley "*saw in the [glaciers] the gradual extinction of all life in the valleys in a smother of 'avalanches, torrents, rocks and thunders*," while the poetic side saw the glaciers as "*a symbol of unutterable and incomprehensible power*" (White 208). To Shelley, the mountain and the glaciers were representative of the greatest power of all, the power of Nature. That power made the mountain not only beautiful, glorious, and majestic, it made the mountain a sort of deity which had the ability to bestow retribution and punishment at will, crushing all life so that the world could be recreated into something better--just as God had destroyed and recreated the world in His attempt to eradicate evil. This further reinforces Shelley's belief that Nature is the seat of true perfection. Obviously, Shelley was awestruck by the sights before, above, and below him that summer day, and these sights provided him with the inspiration for his poem. Once more, we have the majesty and perfection of Nature as the direct influence and stimulus for Shelley's creativity.

"Mont Blanc" is, in essence, a poem about the ability of the human imagination--the seat of creative powers--to realize the ultimate Power of Nature, as represented by the majestic, eternal mountain. When Shelley looked upon the mountain, he realized its power, its knowledge, its eternity, and its perfection, and he--as a man and as a poet--longed to become part of that power, to gain that knowledge, perfection, and, ultimately, that eternity. Shelley, then, likens himself to the "*feeble brook*" which "*will oft assume*" (line 7) the qualities of the mountain when it flows into and mingles with the River Arve. The Poet realizes the power and eternity of the mountain--of Nature--in the opening stanza of the poem, when he says that

> *The everlasting universe of things*
>
> *Flows through the mind, and rolls its rapid waves,*
>
> *Now dark--now glittering--now reflecting gloom--*
>
> *Now lending splendour, where from secret springs*
>
> *The source of human thought its tribute brings*
>
> *Of waters,--with a sound but half its own.* (1-6)

The Poet is also aware of the fact that not only is Nature eternal--rebirth, recreation, occurring every spring--but that, in death, man, too, assumes immortality, through his soul, the essence of his being, which lives forever, and which is guided by Nature toward divine knowledge.

Just as he had longed to glean the secrets of existence from the "*departed dead*" in his youth, he now seeks those secrets from Nature itself. The Poet recognizes that "*strange sleep . . . wraps all in its own deep eternity*" (lines 27-29); most likely, this "*strange sleep*" is none other than death. Compare the lines from "Mont Blanc" to the opening stanza of Queen Mab:

> *How wonderful is Death,*
>
> *Death and his brother Sleep!*
>
> *One, pale as yonder waning moon*

With lips of lurid blue;

The other, rosy as the morn. (1-5)

Shelley tells us here that both death and sleep are likened to elements of Nature: the moon, the dawn, the ocean, and both are deemed "*wonderful*." Further evidence of Shelley's belief in death as that which unveils the great secrets of existence is given in the third stanza of "Mont Blanc," a stanza in which the Poet--Shelley--is drawn ever closer to Nature, and in which his relationship with Nature forms and shapes itself into something almost tangible. In these lines, Shelley states that "*death is slumber*," during which glimpses "*of a remoter world*" are revealed (lines 49-50). In lines which echo many lines in Shelley's work, he asks whether "*some unknown omnipotence unfurled / the veil of life and death*" (lines 53-54), an inquiry which reinforces his conviction that death is really another life, during which all shall be made clear.

Returning to the mountain's power, Shelley then says that "*far, far above, piercing the infinite sky, / Mont Blanc appears*" (lines 60-61), reinforcing the mountain's divine authority and dominion. As in many of Shelley's earliest poems--especially those in his 1809-1813 manuscript notebook--death is likened to sleep, while the power of the mountain is once more lauded as "*some unknown omnipotence*" which momentarily lifts "*the painted veil which those who live / call life*" (1819 "Sonnet," 1-2) and gives the Poet a glimpse of that which lies between life and death. Interestingly, this veil is lifted while the Poet of "Mont Blanc" is in the "*still cave of the witch Posey*" (line 44), who, as Reiman explains, "*personifies the imagination*," and that "*only in the stillness of her cave--within the mind--can the individual communicate with . . . the Universal Mind*" (Poetry and Prose 90).

THE QUEST FOR PERFECTION

In other words, it is only through introspection, through communion with one's self, that one can become close to Nature and thus have communion with Nature itself. By turning inward toward one's own inner thoughts, mind, and soul, and forsaking the outer world of man, one can obtain such glimpses of life's great mysteries--as revealed by Nature--as the Poet experiences in stanza three.

This idea is carried further later in the stanza, when Shelley writes that

> . . . *--all seems eternal now.*
>
> *The wilderness has a mysterious tongue*
>
> *Which teaches awful doubt, or faith so mild,*
>
> *So solemn, so serene, that man may be*
>
> *But for such faith with nature reconciled,*
>
> *Thou hast a voice, great Mountain, to repeal*
>
> *Large codes of fraud and woe; not understood*
>
> *By all, but which the wise, and great, and good*
>
> *Interpret, or make felt, or deeply feel.* (75-83)

The Poet has become, in this passage, a tool of Nature. By partaking of that intimate communion with it, he has been given the ability to become its spokesman; as he says to it, "*Thou hast a voice, great Mountain,*" a voice--Shelley's--to "*repeal*" the falsehoods and misunderstandings long put forth about it by men who have not heard its true voice, men who have "*not understood.*"

The Poet, Shelley, is one of the "*wise, and great, and good*" who have heard its voice, who "*deeply feel*" its power and its message, and who in turn "*interpret, or make felt*" that power and message to all mankind. Poets, like Shelley, who have shared moments of power and revelation with Nature become Nature's voice in a modern, material world which does not connect with it. The Romantic belief that a return to Nature, the seat of true perfection to Shelley, would recreate man as a pure, spiritual being, is clearly seen in the lines of Shelley's poem. The mighty, majestic mountain "*yet gleams on high:--the power is there, / the still and solemn power of mighty sights, / and many sounds, and much of life and death*" (lines 127-129), where "*the secret strength of things / which governs thought, and to the infinite dome / of heaven is as a law, inhabits thee!*" (lines 139-141). As Reiman explains, "*the 'Power' that generates 'things' and is the law of nature also 'governs thought'--mind is ultimately subordinate to the 'remote, serene, and inaccessible' force*" (Poetry and Prose 93) of Nature. Only when man desires that relationship with Nature, the most perfect of all relationships, can he begin to feel the force of Nature working within him, utilizing him for the betterment of his fellow man.

Shelley himself was to continue his own desire for that intimate relationship with Nature through late October of 1819, when he began what has become perhaps his most well-known poem, "Ode to the West Wind." Though the basic imagery and idea of the ode had been with Shelley since 1817 (one first sees it in The Revolt of Islam), and while the ode is, indeed, a call for a peaceful, bloodless revolution, Shelley returns once more to the theme of "A Summer Evening Churchyard," Queen Mab and Alastor. Once more, Shelley is exploring the relationship between man and Nature, this time with greater intensity than he had in the past. "West Wind" uses the imagery of autumn leaves scattering across the earth, heralding the coming winter, yes, but symbolic of the revolution which Shelley hopes will spread over the world, eradicating the evil just as winter kills the summer.

This poem, more than any other, emphasizes the importance Shelley placed on man's relationship to Nature, as well as his continued hopes for a reformation. Just as he had been in the earlier poems, Shelley was directly influenced by Nature, this time the west wind of the Italian autumn. Shelley explains in his note to the poem that he was inspired by a violent storm which he witnessed while in the woods near the Arno river in Florence. Especially awesome to Shelley was the splendid thunder and lightning. He wrote the first draft of his poem while sitting in the woods (Shelley 573). According to the manuscript notebook in which this poem was drafted, the date of this experience in the woods was Monday, October 25, 1819.

The first three stanzas of the poem concern Nature and its elements: stanza I mentions leaves, seeds and buds--the earth; stanza II deals with clouds--the air; stanza III is about the ocean--water. The Poet himself is introduced in stanza IV, a stanza which connects the first three through the Poet's psalm, or prayer, to Nature, in which he says,

> *If I were a dead leaf thou mightest bear,*
>
> *If I were a swift cloud to fly with thee;*
>
> *A wave to pant beneath thy power, and share*

> *The impulse of thy strength, only less*
>
> *Than thou, O uncontrollable! If even*
>
> *I were as in my boyhood, and could be*
>
> *The comrade of thy wanderings over Heaven.* . . . (43-49)

Shelley once more reinforces the connection between death, Nature, and perfection, a connection he had long explored. He longs to be a "*dead leaf*" which Nature would carry. He would also willingly be a cloud, soaring through the sky with Nature, or a wave gasping under the weight of Nature's power. Intriguingly, each of these--the dead leaf, the cloud, the wave--is completely controlled by Nature, leading one to assume that Shelley longed to be controlled and shaped by Nature in the same manner he had long controlled and shaped the women in his life.

The further implication of this interpretation is that his relationship with Nature filled a need within him that no human relationship could ever fulfill. However, like the Poet of Alastor and "Hymn to Intellectual Beauty," Shelley once again desires what is, in reality, unobtainable: the perfect relationship. This time, he prays passionately to be made one with Nature. He is, he says, "*too like*" (line 56) Nature already, a being who is too free, impassioned, and august for the world of man. Neither Nature nor Shelley are understood by mankind; they are, then, separate from the world of mankind. Therefore, they should join forces, whereupon they can instigate the revolution which will create the perfect world. In lines reminiscent of "A Summer Evening Churchyard,"

THE QUEST FOR PERFECTION

<u>Alastor</u>, and the "Hymn," Shelley refers to his youth, when he was "*the comrade of [Nature's] wanderings,*" when he came close to the seat of divinity via the graveyard visits and incantations.

The Poet's prayer to Nature, to be made one with it, takes on a rather demanding, or perhaps desperate, tone in the final stanza:

> *Make me thy lyre, even as the forest is:*
>
> *What if my own leaves are falling like its own!*
>
> *The tumult of thy mighty harmonies*
>
> *Will take from both a deep autumnal tone,*
>
> *Sweet though in sadness. Be thou, Spirit fierce,*
>
> *My spirit! Be thou me, impetuous one!*
>
> *Drive my dead thoughts over the universe*
>
> *Like withered leaves to quicken new birth!* (57-64)

When the stanza opens, Shelley is the instrument of the wind; by the end, the wind is the instrument of Shelley. Since, as we have seen, mankind does not understand nor hear either Shelley or Nature, perhaps their combined voices and powers can make their message heard and understood. This is, then, a co-dependent relationship, each needing the other's power to reach the goal of "*quickening a new birth*"--a revolution for

Shelley, Spring for Nature, though they are both the "*prophecy*" of line 69. Together, they shall bring new life to the world.

Fascinating to note is that the Poet--Shelley--in the first line of the stanza, compares himself to the forest, and then says, "*What if my own leaves are falling like its own.*" Just as dead leaves fall from the trees and are scattered far and wide by Nature's breath, the wind, the Poet's "*leaves*" shall become scattered "*among mankind.*" These leaves, which are, literally, the pages of his poems and pamphlets, contain his message and his plans and hopes for a bloodless revolution and a perfect world. Equally intriguing is the very fact that, as Shelley acknowledges in the poem, only dead leaves fall from their trees and are scattered by the wind. This implies that Shelley's leaves will '*fall*' from his grasp and, with Nature's help, be scattered among man, only after his death; in other words, Shelley seems to realize, whether consciously or not, that his greatest fame will come to him after his death. As in his earlier poems, there is a preoccupation with death, a belief that death shall bring with it a certain degree of security and perfection. Since he had never found complete happiness, understanding, security, and perfection in any of his human relationships, Shelley increasingly turned to Nature for the comfort he could find nowhere in the world of man.

When Shelley addresses the elements of Nature in stanzas I, II, and III, it seems curious, at first, that the most subversive element--fire--is missing. Fire, as naturalits are aware, is both destructive and rejuvenating, often used to completely clear a forest so that fresh, new plant life can find life there. When one reads stanza five, therefore, the confusion ends, for the Poet himself is the fire. When he says, "*by the incantation of this verse, / Scatter, as from an*

THE QUEST FOR PERFECTION

unextinguished hearth / Ashes and sparks, my words among mankind! (lines 65-67), clearly he considers himself (as in <u>Alastor</u>) a member of Nature's family, one of its elements. Now, however, the Poet is not merely a brother in search of answers--he is a force as powerful as Nature itself, a force to be joined with its. And, by the end of the poem, they are joined: "*the breath of the wind becomes the poet's own breath; he assumes its spiritual power*" (Cronin 241). The Poet is ever closer to attaining his highest goal: the intimate relationship with Nature which will, ultimately, impart to him perfection itself. It was Shelley's belief that if he was made part of Nature, he would acquire its qualities and virtues: strength, power, beauty, and perfection.

     Shelley's prayer to be made one with Nature is revisited in "To a Sky-Lark," composed in late June 1820 at Leghorn, where the Shelleys were then staying. Godwin Shelley tells us that her husband was inspired by the singing of a skylark, which he heard during an evening stroll (Shelley 629). As in his earlier poems about Nature, Shelley was directly influenced by the beauty of one of its components. In the first six stanzas, Shelley describes the bird in flight, referring to it as a "*blithe Spirit*" (line 1). In the second part, stanzas 7 through 12, Shelley ponders the true nature of the bird, stating that, "*What thou are we know not; / What is most like thee?*" (lines 31-32), and then comparing it to the poet. In stanzas 13 through 21, Shelley's poem becomes a prayer for the bird to make the Poet one like itself, and for it to "*teach us, Sprite or Bird, / what sweet thoughts are thine*" (lines 61-62). Stanza 17 introduces Shelley's long-held belief that death holds truths which man cannot even imagine:

> *Waking or asleep,*
>
> *Thou of death must deem*
>
> *Things more true and deep*
>
> *Than we mortals dream,*
>
> *Or how could thy notes flow in such a crystal stream?*
> (81-85)

Just as he had written in earlier poems, such as "A Summer Evening Churchyard," Alastor and "Hymn to Intellectual Beauty," Shelley here states that Nature and its children--in this case the bird--know the truths and mysteries which man seeks to know, and that only in death does man find the answers he seeks.

The poem ends in a plea similar to that in "Ode to the West Wind" of the previous year. The Poet asks (or, rather, pleads) to be made like the bird, filled with beautiful songs, for then the people would really listen to what he had to say:

> *Teach me half the gladness*
>
> *That thy brain must know,*
>
> *Such harmonious madness*
>
> *From my lips would flow*
>
> *The world should listen then--as I am listening now.*
> (101-105)

The bird possesses a poetic gift rarer than any produced by man, "*better than all treasures / that in books are found*" (lines 98-

99). The bird is a child of Nature, and its productions are therefore perfect; Shelley, on the other hand, seems to realize that he is merely human, and as such his productions are flawed and lack the perfection of Nature. For this very reason, the bird's song stems from inner joy and happiness, the poet's from sadness; as Shelley says, "*our sweetest songs area those which tell of saddest thought*" (line 90). This line echoes words found in "Ode to the West Wind," in which the Poet says that Nature's "*mighty harmonies / will take from both a deep, autumnal tone, / sweet though in sadness*" (lines 59-61). In the earlier poem, it is only after the Poet positions himself as the "*lyre*" of Nature, as one like the trees of her forest, that sadness enters Nature's song. Now, a year later, himself saddened by too much loss--the political massacre, the deaths of his children--he longs to be made happy and carefree like the bird. Shelley's sadness shall disappear once he becomes part of Nature and absorbs its happiness and perfection.

The relationship between the Poet, death, and Nature was the foundation of Shelley's next major work, <u>Adonais</u>, which was composed at Pisa during May and June of 1821. In the lines of this poem, Shelley confronts the reality of death and the "*possibilities of immortality*" (Cronin 199). In hauntingly prophetic lines, life after death becomes something almost tangible to Shelley, no longer merely an abstract idea or a vehicle for séances, as it was in his earlier poems. More than he ever had before, Shelley seems to be wishing for death--a watery death.

<u>Adonais</u> consists of three discernible sections. In the first (stanzas 1-21), the Poet struggles to come to terms with death while mourning Adonais and the great poets of past ages. In the second section (stanzas 22-40), Shelley focuses

on the harshness of the world, "*the pain of life*" (Cronin 198), and comes to believe that death is preferable to a mortal life of pain and misery, as he intimates in stanza 40, when the dead Adonais has left the world of man and entered a perfect world, where "*envy and calumny and hate and pain*" (line 353), as well as "*the contagion of the world*" (line 356) can never "*torture*" (line 355) Adonais again. In the final section, the Poet, having decided that death and its afterlife are more desirable, makes his escape from this life, to live where Homer (line 30), Dante and Milton (line 36), Chatterton (line 399), Sidney (line 401), Lucan (line 404), and Keats, dwell in eternity. Finally, the Poet is given what he has most desired, for

> *The breath whose might I have invoked in song*
>
> *Descends on me; my spirit's bark is driven,*
>
> *Far from the shore, far from the trembling throng*
>
> *Whose sails were never to the tempest given;*
>
> *The massy earth and sphered skies are riven!*
>
> *I am borne darkly, fearfully afar;*
>
> *Whilst, burning through the inmost veil of Heaven,*
>
> *The soul of Adonais, like a star,*
>
> *Beacons from the abode where the Eternal are.*
>
> (487-495)

Shelley has (prophetically-so) given himself up to "*the breath whose might [he] invoked in song,*" which "*descends on [him]*" in apparent answer to the Poet's prayer in "Ode to the West

Wind." The dead Poet is then "*borne*" away to "*the abode where the Eternal are*"--just as a dead leaf is carried away by the wind. He has become an immortal being, one privy to the truths and mysteries of existence; he has become one of the "*departed dead*" he had called upon in his youth. By paying homage to the great poets and thinkers of the past as he does, Shelley reiterates his belief that immortality is found only in the souls of great men, specifically Poets, a thought intimated in <u>A Defense of Poetry</u>.

Shelley himself sums up the essence of the relationship between the Poet, Nature, and death when he says that

> *He is made one with Nature; there is heard*
>
> *His voice in all her music, from the moan*
>
> *Of thunder, to the song of night's sweet bird;*
>
> *He is a presence to be felt and known.* (370-373)

These words fulfill the prayer of "Ode to the West Wind," in which the Poet longs to be enjoined with Nature. Though the Poet may have a more intimate relationship with this "*great Mother*" than most men do, Shelley once more realizes that it is only in death that the relationship can be fully consummated. Only then, when the Poet is entombed in "*Rome, which is the sepulchre . . . / at once the Paradise, / the grave, the city, and the wilderness*" (lines 424, 433-434), where "*one keen pyramid*" (line 444) stands guard over him, the Poet will "*awaken from the dream of life*" (line 344).

What Shelley has described in these lines is, of course, the Protestant Cemetery, where both Keats and William

Shelley were buried. The Cemetery was a place Shelley considered perfect, for, in his preface to the poem, he remarked that "*it might make one in love with death, to think that one should be buried in so sweet a place*" (Shelley 425). The beauties of ancient Rome, and of Nature, bring Shelley ever closer to desiring death, and burial in the Protestant Cemetery. In this cemetery, Shelley would not only be surrounded by the majesties of Rome and of Nature, he would also be near the final resting place of his favorite child, William Shelley. He would also be near Keats, a poet Shelley considered a genius; thus, two of the great minds would be companions throughout eternity. This cemetery was, then, the perfect resting place for the earthly remains of the "*gentle child*" (line 235), Adonais, who shall now have "*a grave among the eternal*" (line 58). Shelley's belief that life is really death and death is life--that one begins to fully live only after death--receives its most eloquent execution in this, his greatest poem.

Adonais was, in fact, regarded by the poet himself as his greatest achievement, stating his opinion in several letters throughout 1821 and 1822, beginning on June 5, when he told John and Maria Gisborne that "*it is a highly-wrought piece of art, and perhaps better, in point of composition, than anything I have written*" (Ingpen 2: 872, Shelley's emphasis). On June 11, Shelley wrote to his London publisher, Charles Ollier, that "*'Adonais' . . . is little adapted for popularity, but is perhaps the least imperfect of my compositions*" (Ingpen 2: 876). On September 25, he wrote again to Ollier, repeating that "*the 'Adonais,' in spite of its mysticism, is the least imperfect of my compositions. . . .*" (Ingpen 2: 916). Yet another letter to Ollier, dated November 11, found Shelley stating that, "*I confess I should be surprised if that poem were*

THE QUEST FOR PERFECTION

born to an immortality of oblivion" (Ingpen 2: 922). The next mention of the poem is in a letter to John Gisborne dated April 10, 1822, in which Shelley says, "*I know what to think of 'Adonais,' but what to think of those who confound it with the many bad poems of the day, I know not;*" later, in the same letter, he remarks that "*it is absurd in any Review to criticise 'Adonais,' and still more to pretend that the verses are bad*" (Ingpen 2: 953, 955). As these letters indicate, Shelley regarded this poem as his perfect achievement. In his own mind, then, he had, as a poet, attained perfection. The ramification of this assessment is that the poet would surmise that he had nothing further to accomplish; theoretically, if one is at the pinnacle of perfection, where does that leave one to go, and what is there left to fulfill? Once perfection is accomplished, at least in one's mind, then there is nothing left to strive for, there is nothing left to accomplish. Once perfection has been achieved, there is nothing left to do. Therefore, if Shelley had reached that pinnacle as a poet, at least in his own opinion, then he had certainly attained his goal, and left himself with an uncertain path and an undefined role.

If one studies the poetry that succeeded Adonais, Shelley's next path becomes evident: in Hellas and "The Triumph of Life," Shelley echoed the themes, imagery, and ideas of his earlier work. In essence, Shelley returned, as a mature and seemingly-confident poet of 29, to the ideas behind his early work, perhaps to merely record his mature views on those ideas. One is reminded that when Queen Mab was reprinted in a pirated edition in 1821, Shelley was dismayed, writing that, "*I really hardly know what this poem is about. I am afraid it is rather rough*" (Ingpen 2: 913). Of course, as is natural, Shelley had matured and grown as a man and as a poet since those earlier works; his thoughts and ideas had developed and modified themselves throughout the past seven years. Though his basic principles remained steadfast, Shelley was, of course, not the same man who had written Queen Mab and The Revolt of Islam.

In his last poem, "The Triumph of Life," Shelley returns to the relationship between the Poet and Nature, in a manner that is reminiscent of Alastor and which attempts to answer the "*quest for ideal love [in] Epipsychidion*" (Reiman, Poetry and Prose 454). Discontent in his relationships and in his career, Shelley turns back to his earlier works in an attempt to begin anew the search for the perfect relationship. In this poem, the Poet falls into a "*strange trance*" (line 29), whereupon "*a Vision on [his] brain was rolled*" (line 40). The vision is, in fact, a "*triumphal pageant*" (Reiman 454), during which the Poet's questions ("'*And what is this? / Whose shape is that within the car? & why'-- / 'is all here amiss?*'") invoke the spirit of one of the "*departed dead*".

This being answers that the Poet is in the midst of life itself--intriguingly, that life is full of the dead, those who had left the world of man for a better place. The Poet's description of this being is equally intriguing, for he is, in fact, a tree root whose hair is grass and whose eyes are knotholes (lines 180-188). When the Poet inquires as to this being's identity, the reply reveals that this is none other than Rousseau, one who had greatly influenced Shelley; Rousseau--the tree--tells Shelley that,

THE QUEST FOR PERFECTION

>   . . . *'before thy memory*
>
> *'I feared, loved, hated, suffered, did, and died,*
>
> *And if the spark with which Heaven lit my spirit*
>
> *Earth had with purer nutriment supplied*
>
> *'Corruption would not now thus much inherit*
>
> *Of what was once Rousseau--nor this disguise*
>
> *Stain that within which still disdains to wear it.--*
> (199-205)

The captivating implication of these lines is that Rousseau--the proponent of communion with Nature--became, after death, a literal part of Nature. In Shelley's poem he is a tree--a dead tree. Shelley has made Rousseau into what he himself had long desired to be: a dead tree whose leaves, or, words, would be scattered among mankind. Interestingly, this great writer, who is now one of Nature's "*lyres*" is also the one who encourages the Poet--Shelley--to continue his poetic pursuits; he "*warns the Poet against giving way to inaction because of despair by distinguishing relative degrees of resistance to Life's evil influence*" (Reiman, Poetry and Prose 454). Rousseau gives Shelley the courage and the confidence to continue his career as a poet.

Though "The Triumph of Life" remains unfinished, clearly Shelley's self-doubts about his continued ability as a poet prompted the conversation between the Poet and Rousseau in the poem. The discontent Shelley had been feeling as a poet was soothed and allayed by Rousseau, whose ideas had helped form many of Shelley's own ideas. Shelley must have concluded that the only path for him in life was poetry, and the poetic conversation between Shelley and Rousseau was really Shelley's way of encouraging and preparing himself to continue on that path and remain a poet.

Through the poem, Shelley rejuvenated his mind and spirit to continue the mission he had assigned to himself years before: to help mankind recognize that perfection is not only desirable but possible. Shelley had, through the character of Rousseau, alleviated his doubts not only about his role as a poet, but also the possibility of perfection. Alan Weinberg concluded that Shelley was "mentally conditioning" himself for the task of following Rousseau's advice, for "he sees how hard it is to start anew" on his own. This apparent need to find support, comfort, and understanding led Shelley to seek it in Rousseau, a dead poet, rather than a living human being. As he had before, Shelley emphasized the relationship with the dead, rather than the living. Perhaps this was because Shelley was pondering the fate of dead poets.

VI: The Lifting of the Veil: Death and the Poet

Increasingly unhappy in the world of man, Shelley was drawn--in the last year of his life--to the sea, a part of Nature, and ever closer to death. To Shelley, death was the bearer of true perfection, that which allowed one to absorb the perfection of Nature. By becoming embraced, through burial, by Nature, one was able to enter into the most perfect of all relationships, and was led toward divine enlightenment and, ultimately, perfection.

Given Shelley's long-held obsession with death, it seems only natural that Shelley would turn to the sea for comfort when he felt that the world and people had let him down. Shelley never learned how to swim, so one must wonder why, then, he would be willing to spend so many hours sitting calmly in his boat while the waves rolled beneath him. He literally risked his life each time he went out in the Don Juan, his boat, and this leads to the intriguing inquiry as to his intentions: was he simply seeking solace and comfort from the sea, relaxing in its rocking motions, or was he hoping to be swept overboard to certain death? Though we will never know with certainty what Shelley's intentions were, the poetry of his last months reveals that he was preoccupied with death and its afterlife, leading one to assume that he longed to experience that afterlife for himself.

The last months of Shelley's life seem to have been prophesied in his own poetry. During this time, Shelley turned increasingly from human relationships and increasingly toward the sea. This attraction to the water is hauntingly intriguing, for water has long been a literary symbol of rebirth and renewal. Interestingly, Shelley worked on his last poem--a poem in which, as we have seen, his doubts and fears are allayed--aboard his own boat. In fact, Shelley was so drawn to the water and to boating that he moved his group of family and friends to Lerici in order to be closer to the bay of Spezia. The area was so beautiful that Shelley and his friend, Edward Ellerker Williams, spent every possible moment on board their boat (Shelley 670). It was this passion for the sea which was to eventually bring Shelley's life on earth to an end.

The facts of what happened that July 8 are few, but what is known is that Shelley and Williams departed Leghorn, where they had gone to see the Leigh Hunt family safely settled into Byron's residence, only after "*buying supplies for the little colony at San Terenzo--food, milk for the children, and a hamper of wine to be presented to Signor Maglian, the friendly harbor master at Lerici*" (White 461-462). Shelley remained true to his beliefs until the hour of his death, giving to those less fortunate than himself, and trying to better their situation even a little; Shelley showed, as always, that he was concerned with the lives and the fates of his fellow beings. He was a humanitarian until the end of his life. By six o'clock that evening a squall had risen, and their little boat, the Don Juan, was caught in its midst. According to witness accounts and the salvaged remains of the craft, White concluded that "*she had sunk as the result of a collision*," [and]

> *that Shelley's end came very quickly. He would not have had the time, as when he faced drowning in the Chanel in 1816, 'to reflect and even to reason upon*

THE QUEST FOR PERFECTION

> death,' or to reach the conclusion then reached that 'it was rather a thing of discomfort than horror to me.' Byron had seen him resolve to drown rather than risk another's life on Lake Geneva. Trelawny, within the last few months, had been deeply impressed with his indifference both to the idea and to the physical discomfort of dying and had heard him speak of going down with the Don Juan like a piece of ballast in case she wrecked. In poems, letters, and conversations he had shown for several years that he regarded death primarily as a release and an opportunity and that his desire to live was based upon his personal obligations. 'If I die tomorrow,' he had remarked to Marianne Hunt on the previous day, 'I have lived to be older than my father; I am ninety years of age.' It seems certain that he died calmly, probably with little or no effort to save himself. (White 463)

Shelley seems to have increasingly desired death during the last year of his life. He felt obligated to live because of the many people he felt responsibilities for, foremost among them his wife and son; Leigh Hunt, whom he had promised to assist in his literary efforts; and Claire Clairmont, who was emotionally and financially dependent upon him. His concern for other peoples' welfare, then, is what kept him from actively seeking death.

As always, Shelley viewed death as that which frees one from the pain and concerns of this world and gives one the peace and happiness of the perfect world. Though he probably died quickly, and did not have the time to ponder his fate, Shelley was--if one believes his doctrine--finally given that which he most desired: the chance to discover the ultimate Truth, and, perhaps, a new life in a better and perfect world.

When the bodies of Shelley and Williams washed ashore, quarantine laws insisted that they be cremated on the beach. Shelley's cremation occurred August 16, on the beach of the Tuscan Coast. During the ceremony, Hunt remained alone in the carriage, while Byron stood by, "*silent and thoughtful*" (Trelawny 223). As they watched, "*the corpse fell open and the heart was laid bare*" (Trelawny 223) in the flames, and Byron, unable to watch any longer, swam out to sea. Trelawny noticed the frontal bones of the skull and the jaw bone remained unscathed by the flames, "*but what surprised [them] all*," he recalled, "*was that the heart remained entire. In snatching this relic from the fiery furnace [his] hand was severely burnt . . .*" (Trelawny 224). In what easily could have been a scene composed by Shelley himself, his heart, which had been so full of compassion, hope, and poetry, was rescued from the destructive flames, to remain with the people who had meant the most to him.

The heart was to become a symbolic link between the dead, departed Shelley and those left behind in the world of man. The heart was to forever remind those people of Shelley's message of love, hope, and perfection, and the story of its refusal to burn was to similarly inspire generations of readers. Many came to believe that, since Shelley had publicized goodness and perfection during his lifetime, then his heart was endowed with those qualities; its survival upon the funeral pyre served to reinforce Shelley's belief that man is essentially, innately good. Many were thus led to the same belief that the goodness in man can be brought to the forefront, overshadowing the evil side. In death, therefore,

THE QUEST FOR PERFECTION

Shelley accomplished what he had never been able to achieve in life: he was able to fill the hearts of many with the hope that the perfectibility of mankind is, indeed, a possibility.

In deciding Shelley's final resting place, Godwin Shelley and Trelawny looked to <u>Adonais</u> for their answer, choosing a plot under the pyramid of Cestius in Rome's Protestant Cemetery. The heart, however, was not placed in the tomb with the poet's ashes; it was first given to Hunt, who eventually gave it to Godwin Shelley, who kept it wrapped in a copy of <u>Adonais</u>. Shelley's heart was buried in the churchyard of St. Peter's in Bournemouth, in the tomb where Godwin Shelley, Percy Florence, his wife, William Godwin and Mary Wollstonecraft Godwin are buried. Just as he had belonged to two countries--England and Italy--in life, Shelley remains a part of each in death.

Given the nature of Shelley's death in relation to his life-long search for perfection, the student of his life can easily agree with Godwin Shelley when she writes that <u>Adonais</u> is more pertinent to Shelley than to Keats, and that the poem is prophetic regarding Shelley's ultimate fate. She goes on to say that the fame he inherited upon his death would quiet the scornful pens of his many critics (Shelley 656). As Shelley himself had once predicted, his greatest fame came to him in the decades following his death, when he finally gained the readership he had longed to have. His words were garnering the attention they had never had during his life, and his message was being spread among mankind. Interestingly, Shelley's revolutionary message was to be the cornerstone of an 1824 movement instigated by two young Americans--Francis Wright and Robert Dale Owen--which proposed freedom for slaves. Wright and Owen adopted

<u>Queen Mab</u> as their guidebook, and printed the first American edition of the poem in 1831 (St. Clair 479). This was a movement Shelley would have been pleased to participate in, as a lover of freedom, and through the legacy of his work he was able to do so.

Considering that Shelley often referred to life as the veil which separates man from the afterlife, thus making life death and death life, and his early attempts at divining the eternal truths of Nature, one finds it reasonable to view the death he suffered as the ideal, perfect death. His drowning in the sea recalls to mind an incident of 1821, when Shelley--who never learned to swim--tried to swim at Trelawny's encouragement, but failed. Unable to resurface, Shelley made no attempt to save himself; when his friend realized that Shelley was on the verge of drowning, he rescued him, only to have the poet reply that,

> *I always find the bottom of the well, and they say Truth lies there. In another minute I should have found it, and you would have found an empty shell. It is an easy way of getting rid of the body.*

(Trelawny 190)

Not only do these remarks reiterate Shelley's belief that truth, and thus perfection, are found only in death, but they also relate his feeling that death was not, therefore, to be feared.

As his poems and letters illustrate, Shelley regarded death as something mystical, the vehicle which would transport one to Paradise, hence giving birth to a "*world divine*" (Shelley 419), where "*no more [would] Life divide what Death can join together*" (Shelley 438). Shelley's words in <u>Adonais</u> reflect

THE QUEST FOR PERFECTION

his thoughts on death; by emphasizing the beauty of Rome's scenery, Shelley turns the resting place into a camposanto, which in Italian means "holy city," and is used to designate a cemetery (Reiman 405). The cemetery thus becomes a divine place, restating Shelley's belief that death reveals the ultimate truths. The poem also makes reference to the grave of young William Shelley, which was near Keats--and now Shelley. These words are, perhaps, the fittest epitaph one such as Shelley could have:

> *Go thou to Rome,--at once the Paradise,*
>
> *The grave, the city, and the wilderness;*
>
> *And where its wrecks like shattered mountains rise,*
>
> *And flowering weeds, and fragrant copses dress*
>
> *The bones of Desolation's nakedness*
>
> *Pass, till the spirit of the spot shall lead*
>
> *Thy footsteps to a slope of green access*
>
> *Where, like an infant's smile, over the dead*
>
> *A light of laughing flowers along the grass is spread;*
>
> *And gray walls moulder round, on which dull Time*
>
> *Feeds, like slow fire upon a hoary brand;*
>
> *And one keen pyramid with wedge sublime,*
>
> *Pavilioning the dust of him who planned*

> *This refuge for his memory, doth stand*
>
> *Like flame transformed to marble; and beneath,*
>
> *A field is spread, on which a newer band*
>
> *Have pitched in Heaven's smile their camp of death,*
>
> *Welcoming him we lose with scarce extinguished breath.*
>
> . . . .
>
> *The One remains, the many change and pass;*
>
> *Heaven's light forever shines, Earth's shadows fly;*
>
> *Life, like a dome of many-coloured glass,*
>
> *Stains the white radiance of Eternity,*
>
> *Until Death tramples it to fragments.*
>
> (433-450, 460-464)

According to Shelley, life deforms the divine perfection of the supreme Omnipotence--the "*One*"--into "*fragments*" of earthly imperfection. Death is that which restores the perfection and joins the "*departed dead*" with the supreme Omnipotence, thus giving perfection to the dead being. Earth, or, rather, the world of man, destroys the perfection of the "*One*," for perfection cannot exist in the world of man. The imperfect world of man shall eventually fade, like shadows and dreams, into nothingness; only the perfection of Heaven, of Paradise, is eternal.

THE QUEST FOR PERFECTION

The souls of the dead poets, Adonais and Shelley, have been united with the perfection and immortality of the One, and of Heaven, and have thus assumed that perfection and immortality. Until the end of his life, Shelley believed that death was the seat of true perfection, and that one would exist in a state of eternal perfection only after death, when one is entombed within Nature. Upon one's burial, one inherits and absorbs the perfection of Nature; Nature, then, is the vehicle which allows one to be united with the "*One*" in Paradise.

Shelley's belief that perfection lies in death could but lead him to a premature death. His inability to find contentment in a human relationship, his inability to accept that human beings and their creations--including government--are not perfect, and cannot be perfect, led him to suffer continual pain, discouragement, and heartbreak. Because of his ardent belief in, and desire for, perfection, Shelley was unable to live in the world of man. This left him no viable option but to seek death, and whether he let himself die that July day, as some have wondered, Shelley seems to have been consigned to death at a young age. It can be no mere accident that Shelley died at the age of 29, just one month before his thirtieth birthday; he left the world of man before he had a chance to reach middle age, and before he could become old, bitter, and full of disgust at his idealistic ideas and beliefs. Death allowed Shelley to remain the hopeful, idealistic, revolutionary poet.

Death permitted Shelley to escape what he could not accept nor easily deal with: human beings. Shelley was too idealistic to accept that human beings are not perfect, that they do make mistakes, and that they are not always happy and carefree. He refused to appreciate that mankind has a dark side that cannot be denied; to deny the dark side would lead to insanity, for people are not meant to be always good, happy, and unconcerned. The good must be balanced by the bad; otherwise, the good will not be appreciated. Denial of evil--a belief in Shelley's doctrine--leads one to suffer the same fate as Shelley: certain death. Though death should not be neurotically feared, neither should it be desired and sought.

In remaining a member of the human race, one can utilize his or her life and talents for the betterment of the world and of mankind. One should not follow Shelley's doctrine, believing that death is the answer, for death brings a certain end to life on earth, where one can help instigate change. On earth, people can do their part for mankind, nature, and society's institutions: helping those less fortunate, becoming environmentally aware, or being politically active; in doing so, one shall be perpetuating, in the most perfect way, the best of Shelley's philosophy.

NOTES

1. Perfection, as defined by Shelley's doctrines and beliefs, contained the best of man and of nature. His belief that mankind could be restored and recreated as a sinless, good being--such as Adam and Eve had been before the introduction of sin into the Garden of Eden--led him to deny that evil was a natural part of human beings and of the world, including nature. The flaw in Shelley's belief is this very denial of evil, thus making his hopes and ideas impossible to achieve, and condemning him to suffer the very things he longed to eradicate from the world: pain, frustration, and heartbreak.

2. Shelley defined art as any creative production of human beings, including literature, painting, sculpture, music, and dance.

3. Shelley advanced free love as the perfect alternative to marriage, an institution to which he strongly objected. Shelley felt that it was highly unjust to restrict and control two free, independent spirits with the legalities of marriage. Shelley believed that, since no one can predict how they shall feel towards another in the future, they should not be obligated to remain in a marriage because they are legally bound to do so. Shelley felt that, as one's feelings changed, they should be free to move on to the next relationship. In fact, Shelley detested marriage because it prevented either or

both partners from simply walking away from the relationship once the love was gone (Cameron, Young Shelley 78-79, 266).

Shelley's views on religion were equally unorthodox. In fact, Shelley, at different stages in his life, referred to himself as a deist and an atheist. An examination of his body of works, including his letters, however, reveals that he was actually a deist and an infidel: Shelley believed in a Divine Creator, while at the same time, he felt that this Creator did not have total control over the destiny of the world and of man. As we have seen, Shelley believed that mankind could take control of his own fate, that he could change the course of history, and that he could perfect himself and his world. In my opinion, Shelley used the term "atheist" as a means of both communicating his renunciation of orthodox Christian beliefs, and of attempting to encourage others to think for themselves and come to their own conclusions about religion.

Shelley was also unable to accept that the Christian God could create both good and evil. Something that is supposedly as good and perfect as God would not be able to create evil. Satan, a being battling for control of mankind, created evil in order to tempt mankind to follow him. Once mankind had fallen prey to his promises of wealth and power, mankind became infected with greed, selfishness, and cruelty, and evil was thus introduced into the world. Furthermore, Shelley objected to the control exerted over religion by the monarchy and the aristocracy; their beliefs were to be the beliefs of everyone, erasing free will from the very heart of religion. When Elizabeth Hitchener wrote to Shelley on religion, he replied that

THE QUEST FOR PERFECTION

> *the religion of the Deist, or the worshipper of virtue would suffice, without involving the persecution, battles, bloodshed, which countenancing Christianity countenances.--I think, my friend, we are the devoutest professors of true religion I know, --if the perverted and prostituted name of 'religion' is applicable to the idea of devotion to Virtue. 'The just man made perfect' I doubt not of: but to this simple truth where is the necessity of annexing fifty contradictory dogmas, in order that men may destroy each other to know what is right?* (Ingpen 1: 167)

As is clear from this letter, Shelley also objected to the manipulation of religion by self-serving rulers. He also resented the contradictions between different branches of Christianity, contradictions which would only lead to the confusion and ultimate manipulation of the people. To Shelley, organized religion was merely a means by which the rulers and leaders controlled and brainwashed their subjects, usually in the wars begun by these leaders. Shelley could not reconcile the violent loss of life with Christianity's messages of hope, love, and peace.

4. Shelley viewed marriage as an unnecessary institution of mankind, an institution which could prevent one from following his emotions. Marriage was the antithesis of a happy relationship, for it forced two people to remain together even if, or when, their love had faded. Despite the fact that he detested marriage, Shelley did marry twice. He was able to justify and reconcile his compromise, for he felt it "*best, in the interest of happiness, to submit to the dictates of society*"

(Cameron, Young Shelley 266). Probably because of the reactions received when he ran away with Harriet Westbrook--they were, after all, young, unmarried, unchaperoned, traveling across England and Scotland together--Shelley realized that it was best for Westbrook if they marry. Otherwise, she would have been ostracized from society, something, Shelley recognized, she would have found unbearable. Though he compromised his belief in free love, and his convictions against marriage, Shelley typically considered Westbrook's situation in deciding to marry her. However, Shelley did not allow the legalities of marriage to keep him bound to her, for when he fell out of love with her, and in love with Mary Wollstonecraft Godwin, he left his wife to be with his new love. Obviously, both Shelley and Wollstonecraft Godwin suffered harshly during this time, and, upon Westbrook's suicide, they married to escape the criticism and condemnation of society.

WORKS CONSULTED

Adams, Simon, John Briquebec, and Ann Kramer. <u>Illustrated Atlas of World History</u>. New York: Random House, 1992.

Cameron, Kenneth Neill, ed. <u>Shelley and His Circle</u>. Vol. II. Cambridge: Harvard U Press, 1961.

--------. <u>The Young Shelley</u>. New York: The Macmillan Company, 1950.

Cronin, Richard. <u>Shelley's Poetic Thought</u>. New York: St. Martin's Press, 1981.

Hawkins, Desmond. <u>Shelley's First Love</u>. Hamden CT.: Archon Books Inc., 1992.

Holmes, Richard. <u>Shelley: The Pursuit</u>. New York: Penguin Books, 1987.

Ingpen, Roger, ed. <u>The Letters of Percy Bysshe Shelley</u>. 2 vols. London: Sir Isaac Pitman & Sons, Ltd., 1909.

Jones, F.L., ed. <u>Mary Shelley's Journal</u>. Norman, OK: U of Oklahoma Press, 1947.

Peacock, Thomas Love. "Memoirs of Shelley." <u>The Life of Percy Bysshe Shelley</u>. Vol. II. London: J.M. Dent and Sons Limited, 1933.

Reiman, Donald H., ed. <u>The Esdaile Notebook</u>. The Manuscripts of the Younger Romantics: Percy Bysshe

Shelley, Vol. I. New York: Garland Publishing, Inc., 1985.

--------, ed. <u>Shelley and His Circle</u>. Vol. VI. Cambridge: Harvard U Press, 1973.

-------- and Susan B. Powers, eds. <u>Shelley's Poetry and Prose</u>. New York: W.W. Norton & Company, 1977.

Shelley, Percy Bysshe. <u>The Complete Poetical Works of Percy Bysshe Shelley</u>. Thomas Hutchinson, ed. London: Oxford U Press, 1927.

St. Clair, William. <u>The Godwins and the Shelleys: The Biography of a Family</u>. New York: W.W. Norton, 1989.

Trelawny, Edward John. "Recollections of the Last Days of Shelley and Byron." Vol. 2 of <u>The Life of Percy Bysshe Shelley</u>. London: J.M. Dent and Sons Limited, 1933. 2 vols.

Weinberg, Alan. "Shelley's Humane Concern and the Demise of Apartheid." Shelley Bicentennial Conference. New York Public Library, May 22, 1992.

White, Newman Ivey. <u>Portrait of Shelley</u>. New York: Alfred A. Knopf, 1945.

Woodring, Carl R. <u>Prose of the Romantic Period</u>. Boston: Houghton Mifflin Company, 1961.

ACKNOWLEDGMENTS

I love to learn; I always enjoyed being a student. I thrive when steeped in books and research. No part of my academic experience has exceeded the semester I spent researching and writing my graduate thesis. For years I had anticipated graduate school with awe and wonder, mostly because I would finally have the chance to spend five months immersed in my favorite literary figure: Percy Bysshe Shelley.

Over the preceding years, I had read everything I possibly could about Shelley. I formed my own thoughts about the man and the poet, and those thoughts formed the basis for my focus and scope. No academic pursuit has ever felt as passionate, true, meaningful, and joyful for me.

In the years since I wrote this thesis, people continued to encourage me to seek its publication—to send my leaves into the world, upon Shelley's West Wind. Colleagues, friends, even students, all said I should add my thoughts and feelings about Shelley to the already extensive number of books written about this young man. I have finally done so.

I may not have published this work without the perennial nudges and requests to do so. Collective gratitude, then, extends to all of those professors—those who guided me and those who have been my colleagues—friends, family members, and students past and present, all of whom voiced interest in seeing this book out in the world. Thank you for your faith, positivity, and encouragement.

www.ingramcontent.com/pod-product-compliance
Lightning Source LLC
Chambersburg PA
CBHW021410290426
44108CB00010B/472